LESSONS FROM THE TROUBLES AND THE UNSETTLED PEACE

Ideas from the Forward Together podcasts

Edited by Paul Gosling from
original interviews undertaken as the
'Forward Together' podcasts

**HOLYWELL
TRUST**

Published October 2020 by
Holywell Trust
10-14 Bishop Street
Derry/Londonderry BT48 6PW
T: (028) 7126 1941
www.holywelltrust.com

ISBN 978 1 9997566 1 1

Layout/design by Joe McAllister, Colmcille Press
www.colmcillepress.com

"The debate that needs to happen is the debate between people with ideas."
Senator Mark Daly

CONTENTS

INTRODUCTION

The ideas in this book emerged from the Forward Together programme of work conducted by the Holywell Trust, led by Gerard Deane, in which 35 leading thinkers considered how to make progress in Northern Ireland. Those interviewed ranged from community and religious leaders to senior politicians. Their proposals for action went far beyond what we, as programme initiators, expected. We don't want those ideas to be lost – especially as Northern Ireland's politics show only stuttering progress and a lack of willingness to commit to genuine partnership.

We asked people four questions: 'How can we strengthen civic society?'; 'How do we build a shared and integrated society?'; 'How can we deal with the past in ways that aid, not hinder, reconciliation?'; and 'How can we have the constitutional conversation without creating new division and tension?'. We hope that you will agree with us that the answers were not only interesting, but also challenging. They were the result of serious consideration. In return they warrant serious consideration by the population of Ireland as a whole and, in particular, by Northern Ireland's decision-makers and opinion-formers.

Observations and proposals are broken down into 12 key themes – which go far beyond the four core questions that we asked. Those 12 themes are central to how we make progress. The one point that no one disagreed on was that we do need to make progress – 22 years on from the Good Friday Agreement we have to continue to take peace seriously, accelerate the reform of our public services and take stronger action to bind our society together.

Interviews took place during a long period of suspension of the Executive and Assembly, which, happily, has now been replaced by a functioning government, albeit one characterised by continuing mutual distrust. Each chapter can be read on its own: consequently, some key points are repeated.

The original Forward Together Series 1 podcast interviews are available for listening, along with Series 2, at the Holywell Trust website, https://www.holywelltrust.com/forward-together.

Setting the Context

The interviews in series one of the Forward Together podcasts were conducted towards the end of a long period of Assembly and Executive suspension. The institutions were restored after the *New Decade, New Approach* deal was brokered by the most interventionist secretary of state – Julian Smith – that Northern Ireland has benefited from for a long time. Despite this, he was sacked soon after.

New Decade, New Approach addressed some of the residual problems that had beset the institutions, notably the petition of concern and the lack of progress with the promised Bill of Rights. But it failed to deal with other matters, such as the designation arrangements within Stormont.

There is an assumption that peace has been secured and permanent. Several interviewees made the point that we are only mid-way through what is likely to be a 50-year peace process. Some commented that its continuation is not guaranteed.

It is worth considering some worrying parallels with Lebanon – another society ravaged by internal conflict that lasted for a protracted period. The negotiated solution in Lebanon, like Northern Ireland, was achieved by the main religious/communal factions being brought together in government. But, as in Northern Ireland, those factions continued in government to focus on their own narrow interests, rather than governing in true partnership. Armed militias still functioned – which has some similarity to the ongoing existence of some paramilitary groups in Northern Ireland. While the parallels should not be over-stated, they are worrying. Lebanon has dissolved into disorganisation, with the capital city Beirut suffering a serious explosion as the result of institutional failures.

There is a lesson from Lebanon, though, which is also the lesson from Northern Ireland's own past – progress is not inevitable, nor is it continuous. It has to be worked at. Political advances need to lead to social and economic progress that is felt across society. While *New Decade, New Approach* certainly takes Northern Ireland society forward, the observations from our interviewees represent important ideas on how Northern Ireland can become a better and fairer society: one that is less likely to return to armed conflict.

Paul Gosling / September 2020

ACKNOWLEDGEMENTS

The Forward Together project was an initiative of the Holywell Trust. The project was initially funded by the Community Relations Council, with further development – including the production of this book – financed by the Irish Government's Department of Foreign Affairs through their Reconciliation Fund.

The contributions of the funders is greatly appreciated. The book would not be possible without their assistance – nor, of course, from those opinion formers who agreed to be interviewed.

Thanks are given, of course, to Gerard Deane and Eamonn Deane at Holywell Trust, to Audrey Magowan for correcting the automated transcription of the interviews and for Zoë Weyrauch-Gosling for proof corrections.

Disclaimer:
This project has received support from the Northern Ireland Community Relations Council which aims to promote a pluralist society characterised by equity, respect for diversity, and recognition of interdependence. The views expressed do not necessarily reflect those of the Community Relations Council.

Future projects

The Holywell Trust is committed to further programmes of engagement that promote peace and reconciliation. The Forward Together project continues, with a conference to coincide and complement this book. Original conversations that were published as podcasts remain available from the Holywell Trust website, https://www.holywelltrust.com/forward-together

Holywell Trust delivers a range of other programmes, including:

Future Leaders – a programme (funded through the Reconciliation Fund) to build a new cohort of community leaders, with 20 participants trained each year in a range of areas who will facilitate good relations programmes in the local community.

Holywell Good Relations Programme - a range of interconnected activities to tackle prejudice and discrimination and build relationships. Activities include Human Library, Teatime Events and City Centre Forum events.

Shared Community Building - Holywell Trust is the lead partner of the DiverseCity Community Partnership - a collective of eight community organisations based in a shared building. The building has 11 dedicated spaces for public use from intimate spaces for one-to-one conversations to a large event space that can accommodate up to 110 people and adjoins the Garden of Reflection, a shared public space which, like our building is designed to bring people together.

Garden of Reflection – Summer programme to animate the Garden of Reflection space to the rear of the Holywell building in the heart of Derry/Londonderry - bringing people from all backgrounds together to participate in activities.

Holywell STEW - an initiative to encourage local philanthropic giving and increased community involvement through support for a number of small local projects.

Strabane Shared Space – A Peace IV tender from Derry City and Strabane District Council – a project that has four interconnected elements – Partnership Development Programme, Music Programme, Cemetery Programme and Women's Peacebuilding Programme.

Fingerpost - Holywell is reimagining Derry's community magazine as a website, podcast and series of interconnected events initially examining six community relations and peacebuilding themes.

Investing in Community Leadership in the West - a five year programme with Fermanagh Trust and Rural Community Network addressing community leadership succession planning and skills development.

CONTRIBUTORS

Clare Bailey MLA
Clare Bailey is Green Party MLA for South Belfast and leader of the Green Party in Northern Ireland.

Senator Frances Black
Frances Black is an independent senator in the Oireachtas and at the time of the interview a member of the Oireachtas Good Friday Implementation Committee. She is best known as a successful singer and musician. She established the Rise Foundation, a charity addressing addiction issues.

Denis Bradley
Denis Bradley was co-chair (with Robin Eames) of the Consultative Group on the Past in Northern Ireland. He is former vice chair of the Northern Ireland Policing Board and a former Catholic priest.

Julieann Campbell
Julieann Campbell edited the 'Unheard Voices' collection of women's stories from the Troubles. Julieann is now studying with the Transitional Justice Initiative, examining alternative justice and conflict storytelling.

Senator Mark Daly
Mark Daly is a Fianna Fáil senator, a former chair of the Oireachtas Good Friday Implementation Committee and is currently Cathaoirleach of Seanad Éireann.

Alexandra De La Torre
Alexandra De La Torre co-ordinates parts of The Next Chapter for NICVA, the Northern Ireland Council for Voluntary Action.

Mark Durkan
Mark Durkan has been Northern Ireland's deputy first minister, leader of the SDLP, an MLA and MP for the Foyle constituency, as well as MEP candidate for Fine Gael.

Professor Jim Dornan
Jim Dornan is a former director of fetal medicine at the Royal Maternity Hospital in Belfast and holds professorships with both Queen's University Belfast and Ulster University.

Lord Robin Eames
Robin Eames was co-chair (with Denis Bradley) of the Consultative Group on the Past in Northern Ireland. From 1986 to 2006 he was the Church of Ireland's Archbishop of Armagh and Primate of All Ireland from 1986 to 2006. He now sits in the House of Lords as a life peer.

Jo Egan

Jo Egan is a playwright and the dramatist of 'The Crack in Everything', a performance that was part of the Playhouse's Theatre and Peace Building Academy, financed by the EU's Peace IV programme.

Linda Ervine

Linda Ervine is a community worker within the Turas Project at the Skainos Centre in a strongly loyalist part of East Belfast, where she runs Irish language classes.

Philip Gilliland

Philip Gilliland is a solicitor, practising Anglican and former President of Londonderry Chamber of Commerce.

Ken Good

Ken Good was the Church of Ireland Bishop for the cross-border diocese of Derry and Raphoe at the time of the interview. He has since retired. Ken was born in Cork.

Simon Hamilton

Simon Hamilton was at the time of the interview a DUP MLA, but has since resigned to become chief executive of the Belfast Chamber of Trade and Commerce. He is a former Northern Ireland finance minister, health minister and economy minister.

Maureen Hetherington

Maureen Hetherington is director of The Junction, based in Derry/ Londonderry, a project committed to ethical and shared remembering.

Avila Kilmurray

Avila Kilmurray is working with the Social Change Initiative on peacebuilding work. She is a former director of the Community Foundation for Northern Ireland and was a founder member of the Northern Ireland Women's Coalition.

Cllr John Kyle

John Kyle is a Progressive Unionist Party councillor in Belfast, a former leader of that party and was a GP until his recent retirement.

Naomi Long

Naomi Long is leader of the Alliance Party and is now an MLA and the justice minister of Northern Ireland. At the time of the interview she was also a newly elected MEP, but that position ended with the UK leaving the EU. She has also been MP for East Belfast.

Sophie Long

Sophie Long oversees a sustainable development grants programme in Northern Ireland for a major charity and has been an election candidate for the Progressive Unionist Party, for which she has also been a press officer. She holds a PhD in politics from Queen's University Belfast.

Alan McBride

Alan McBride is a victims' campaigner and a former member of the Northern Ireland Human Rights Commission and the Civic Forum.

Freya McClements

Freya McClements is co-author, with Joe Duffy, of 'Children of the Troubles' and is northern correspondent for the Irish Times.

Andrew McCracken

Andrew McCracken is chief executive of The Community Foundation Northern Ireland.

Conal McFeely

Conal McFeely is chief executive of Creggan Enterprises, which owns and manages the Ráth Mór Centre, a not-for-profit retail and business centre in Derry/Londonderry.

Aideen McGinley

Aideen McGinley is a trustee of Carnegie UK and Co-Chair of its Embedding Wellbeing Project in Northern Ireland. She is a former permanent secretary in the Northern Ireland Civil Service and was chief executive of Fermanagh District Council and of the Ilex Urban Regeneration Company in Derry/Londonderry.

John McKinney

John McKinney was chief executive of the Special European Union Programmes Body and is also a former chief executive of Omagh District Council.

Maeve McLaughlin

Maeve McLaughlin is manager of the Conflict Transformation Peacebuilding Project, also called 'The Derry Model', which is based in the Bloody Sunday Museum. She is a former Sinn Féin MLA and councillor.

Father Martin Magill

Father Martin Magill is a Catholic priest based on the Falls Road in West Belfast. He is a member of the Stop Attacks Forum.

Tina Merron

Tina Merron is chief executive of the Integrated Education Fund.

Mike Nesbitt MLA

Mike Nesbitt is the former leader of the Ulster Unionist Party and remains an MLA. He is a former Northern Ireland victims' commissioner and has been a television presenter.

CHAPTER ONE
THE LEADERSHIP VACUUM

"We have to be leaders and bring people with us."
Claire Sugden MLA

Northern Ireland was without a devolved government for more than three years. The commitment by Westminster and Whitehall to devolution meant that direct rule was not imposed. But the former Secretary of State Julian Smith achieved what his predecessors – Karen Bradley, James Brokenshire and Theresa Villiers – could not and were criticised over. Smith brokered a deal which overcame the political stalemate and got a functioning government back up and running at Stormont.

The interviews contained in this book were conducted during the Assembly's suspension, leading our interviewees to refer to a vacuum of leadership. One consideration was whether only politicians can fill that vacuum, or whether people within civic society can fill the void. Even with the resumption of Stormont, that proposal needs to be kept in mind – the Assembly is not yet an institution we can be confident is durable and stable in uncertain times.

Claire Sugden, the independent unionist MLA and former justice minister, said that her constituents regularly complained at the lack of progress in bringing back Stormont earlier. "The anger amongst the general public is palpable. I feel it and see it every day. What frustrates me is that they assume MLAs are not doing anything. But you know, had they known what we do - whether that's conversations outside of the chamber, whether it's progressing policy in a way that we can because we're scrutinising or holding things to account - they may not feel as angry and it may be a way of helping move the process along.

"I'm a great believer that leadership is about bringing people with you. I don't think politics is doing that right now. How we do it is by informing people and educating them to what their civic duty is as members of the public. Indeed, what the system is that they're voting for and not voting for. That's how we generally move politics forward.

"People talk to me about, 'it's our deeply divided society'. Yes, I suppose that plays a part in hindering our progress, but good politics and good governance is what's missing from our puzzle. The past 20 years were about establishing the institutions, establishing the peace and ensuring that we can get to a place where we can work together. Now is the time when we work together and start delivering for the people of Northern Ireland. When we do that we might start to see that people realise we're all the same despite our backgrounds. We're all aiming for the same thing. I think that's happiness. There's not one person in Northern Ireland that wouldn't tell me they just want to be happy and want the country to move forward. How we get there is leadership and good governance."

Claire is clear that despite the criticisms, the Assembly has been effective and has done good things – just not enough of them, especially when it comes to community cohesion and reconciliation. "It's unfair to say that the Northern Ireland Assembly wasn't working because we're still very unique and it's still a very fractured society". She adds: "it worked for 10 years and [we made] progress, we maybe weren't putting through policies that other jurisdictions were, but we're post-conflict and we should always be viewed in that way.... What often happens with peace processes is we get the peace and then think, 'That's it, we're fixed', and then they [the external intermediaries] move on, when really the most critical part is the post-conflict era because that's ensuring that we actually don't go back to where we were. That's the hard part."

The real challenge, Claire suggests, is how we get the political parties working together. "My experience with the political parties, and I certainly don't speak for any of them, is that they do want to represent the best interests of all the people of Northern Ireland. Every MLA will tell you that it's not just unionists who come into their office, or nationalists, or neither, but it's people from all backgrounds because on a day-to-day, it's our job to represent and advocate on their best interests and behalf. Where we get stuck is on party policy.

> "Maybe if politicians learned to say, 'I made a mistake', put their hands up said they're sorry, maybe we wouldn't find ourselves in the situation we're in."

"Maybe if politicians learned to say, 'I made a mistake', put their hands up said they're sorry, maybe we wouldn't find ourselves in the situation we're in.... sometimes we just need to get back to reality, realising that the job here [in Stormont] is to represent the people of Northern Ireland and try and fight for their best interests. Yes, we all have our own ideological beliefs, we all have our own utopias. Is that really what our job is? I would like to think I'm a very realistic and practical politician and I see my job as about improving public services for the people of Northern Ireland. I think sometimes the higher level stuff gets in the way when really it doesn't affect people on a day-to-day."

Failing to resolve the problems of government – health and education are obvious examples – should lead to politicians thinking seriously about their responsibility to resolve the challenges and improving the lives of individual constituents. Claire says: "I think the greatest skill any politician can have is empathy. You don't have to agree. And I think sometimes we misunderstand empathy with agreement.... To move forward is key, because this past two years has inflamed anger and the people who perhaps have every right to be angry because of what happened to them or their families during our conflict were beginning to move forward, because they didn't want their future generations, and their children, their grandchildren to feel the same way as they do.

"But it almost feels like we're taking the peace process [for granted]", she says, referencing the long Stormont suspension. "So the hard fought peace and the pain and the hurt which endures in many, has almost been brought to the surface again because what was it all for? What was the Good Friday Agreement for? What were the hard decisions that were taken at that time for? And many people, I suppose even from my own perspective and I wasn't of the age to be able to agree to it, but my parents did, there was things within the Good Friday Agreement that I wouldn't have been comfortable with. But it was what we had to do to secure peace and to secure governance and secure a future for Northern Ireland. This past two years if anything have said, 'What was it all for?'. I suppose we made sacrifices whenever we signed the Good Friday Agreement with the hope that it would bring prosperity and peace and now 20 years later it hasn't. It has at least brought peace, but it could go back."

She adds: "The most important descriptor of myself as a politician is 'representative'. Sometimes we have to take our own prejudices outside of what this role is. We have to be leaders and bring people with us. I have so many respectful conversations with people who disagree with me, but it's not about the disagreeing, it's about having the conversation.... The big problem with where we're at now is more to do with relationships than it is issues."

> "It almost feels like we're taking the peace process for granted."

Father Martin Magill, parish priest on the Falls Road in Belfast, observes: "Politics is too important to be left to the politicians alone." And Denis Bradley - co-chair of the Consultative Group on the Past in Northern Ireland and former vice chair of the Northern Ireland Policing Board - believes that our ambitions as a society are too limited – as if the absence of conflict is sufficient. "It's almost as if many of the structures that we created were focused on bringing politics to a place we all could live with - if they got 50%, somebody else would get 50%. But the outflow of that is that we have ended up with institutions and a civil service that don't function particularly well."

But Denis adds that it would be wrong to be over-critical of politicians for this. "I don't completely blame them for that. There's many ways in which we stand on the shoulders of the Good Friday Agreement, but there's even a greater way in which we stand on the shoulders of Anglo-Irish relationships.

"And Anglo-Irish relationships have gone off kilter. And they went off kilter for a couple of reasons. First of all they went off because [the two governments'] assessment was leave the north to mature. Let the politicians, even if they fight with each other, even if they don't do good governance, we will stand behind, we will stand slightly at a distance from that and we'll only come in at the last moment and we'll let them grow in on themselves and learn to be amongst each other." He adds: "Then Brexit was an added unforeseen factor that blew the ship way out of the sea".

John Kyle, a Belfast City Councillor and former leader of the Progressive Unionist Party, observes: "We have a fairly vibrant civil society in Northern Ireland already, but it does seem to exist in a parallel world to the political society or the politicians, which is a problem. And politicians seem to be able to cocoon themselves away from the views, opinions, advice of civil society. Politicians seem to have tin ears when it comes to responding to what broader civil society is saying because there is a huge disparity between what people say they would like to see happen and what politicians are actually doing.

"People need to have the courage to vote outside of their traditional patterns of voting, particularly in elections where the constitutional issue is not at stake, or is not fundamental to what they're doing. We need to realise that we need a broader political representation - people feel exasperated with the politicians who currently hold power, yet they tend to go back and still vote for them at the next election. So people need to have the courage, we need to start a narrative which challenges people to think outside of their traditional habits."

John adds that there is a sense of "people wanting something different yet they keep on doing the same thing". He argues: "politicians clearly are not listening and politicians being politicians they will not listen until it hurts them at the polling booth, at the ballot box. "We can't expect things to change really until it begins to affect who gets elected and that's why people need to stand back, reconsider who they vote for and begin to break some old habits."

He continues: "We need leadership. The problem is that [during the Stormont suspension] we're not getting leadership from our politicians, so other people need to step up and show leadership and our church leaders could do it, but I think that they're not doing that at the present time. I think that our trade unionists could do it. Our business leaders could do it. Our artists, the people in the creative industries, they can also contribute. There are people who are making a difference who are showing leadership but there are too few of them and people perhaps don't realise that they can do it, actually that there is a vacuum of leadership and it just takes some people to step forward and to do it and to show leadership and to begin to say, 'You know, this situation is unacceptable. This behaviour is inappropriate'. This is something that we need to be moving toward as a society and be prepared to take the brickbats and the criticism and the ridicule for doing it, but we need people to do it."

Peter Sheridan – chief executive of the Co-operation Ireland charity and a former assistant chief constable of both the PSNI and the RUC – argues that we must accept that Northern Ireland remains in the early stages of a long period of transition. (A similar point was made by several interviewees.)

He says: "Despite the fact that we are 20 years after the Good Friday Agreement, we are still an immature political society. We still have very micro thinking in terms of how a government should work and the government should be there to protect all of the people's rights. Maybe it's not a surprise, coming out of conflict where people lived like enemies, they now have to learn to live together like citizens. We haven't matured to a place yet that we genuinely want to understand how you protect your neighbour's rights."

Consideration of those rights requires generosity and mutuality, suggests Peter. "Some of that is a top down and some of it is bottom up. One of the frustrations I have is that our political system is such that even when they're in a shared Executive, they all champion their own side's rights. So they set about, 'It's my right to parade', 'It's my right to protest', and what we don't do is look at the other person's rights and good rights. Good rights are where you seek to protect your neighbour's rights, not just your own rights.

"I would want to know from the DUP, 'What is it you are going to do that protects the Catholic tradition, the nationalist tradition, the republican traditions, its cultures and its identity?'. And from Sinn Féin, 'What is it you're going to do that protects the Protestants, unionist, loyalist traditions, their culture and their identity?'.

"One of the weaknesses of the Good Friday Agreement was that we managed to get all of the political parties in Northern Ireland to concede to the British government of Tony Blair. We managed to get them all to concede to the Irish government of Bertie Ahern. We managed to get them all to concede to the American government, of Bill Clinton. But they didn't concede to each other. They got into the Executive and we lost those three people all at the one time and the new prime ministers and Taoiseachs didn't own the baby the same and didn't adopt it to the same extent as the people who were there at the architecture of it. So then our local parties got in and they simply sat and fought for their own rights.

"Until we mature, until political parties start to mature, to sit down and say, 'What would I legislate that would help protect that Catholic, nationalist, republican identity? What would I legislate that would help protect the Protestant traditions, its culture and identity?'. That includes what would they legislate to protect their rights to parades and loyal orders and so on. It might be completely countercultural to somebody's viewpoint on it, but that's where we have to get to."

Peter suggests examples, beginning with the Irish language. "If you understand the Catholic / nationalist / republican tradition, the Irish language is an important part of that identity and culture. If you're on the other side of the fence and maybe you don't have the same understanding but if you want to protect those rights of your neighbour, then you would set about legislating. And similarly, loyal order parades and areas they can't march in are a big issue for loyalist and unionist communities. So it is the practical application of it, it's not about words."

It is up to politicians to show leadership by bringing our society together, argues, Irish language activist Linda Ervine, who is based in loyalist Newtownards Road. "We've got to reach across the divide," she says. "Sadly 20 years after the Good Friday Agreement we are still very much a divided community, which frustrates me greatly. There's been a change in narrative. We have become less sectarian where it's about religion and become more sectarian where it's become about politics.

"The game now is to vilify people because of their politics. Unfortunately, that's played out by our politicians because it sadly works well to polarise people. So it is [essential] to educate young people to realise that because somebody disagrees with you, it doesn't make them the devil. They have an entitlement to a different point of view. We can still build a Northern Ireland that works and build on the good peace work that has been going on for the last years."

Many women believe that the Northern Ireland peace process has not worked for them, despite the central role in the peace process of the Women's Coalition and women having held many of the key leadership positions in Northern Ireland in recent years, as secretaries of state as well as UK prime minister, first minister, deputy first minister and currently leaders of three of the five largest political parties. But, say some, that doesn't inevitably lead to women's priorities being taken into account.

"We have, yes, women on the top of politics, but the question is, are these women representing other women, or are they representing the male orientated politics of their political parties?," asks Alexandra De La Torre, who co-ordinates parts of The Next Chapter for NICVA, Northern Ireland Council for Voluntary Action. She continues: "They are very different things. [It is] one thing to have critical mass. Number two is having women that represent and benefit other women. In Northern Ireland we don't have a childcare strategy, but it is happening in [GB]. Why is it not happening here, when we have women in power? It's not enough having women in power: it's [about] having sufficient power and having women that will work for women."

Maureen Hetherington is director of The Junction, a project committed to ethical and shared remembering. She says: "In any society we need a top down and a bottom up approach." She adds that during the Assembly's suspension, it became even more important for civil society to demonstrate leadership from the bottom up. "Whenever we have politicians who have absolutely no interest in dealing with the common or greater good and everything is based on the self-interest of the party, it becomes stymied and limited. I worry all the time that we raise expectations in the community and then when nothing comes of it, people get very disillusioned, disheartened and they disengage."

> "In any society we need a top down and a bottom up approach."

Maureen echoes points made by Peter Sheridan and Claire Sugden about the maturity of Northern Ireland's political system. "Our deeply segregated society, the way that our politicians behave to each other and with each other, it's hugely contentious and creates a lot of ill feeling," she says. "It's done deliberately in coming up to voting times - that level of hostility goes up. I have to accept there isn't a level of maturity in the political world here

- it takes a generation or two generations before you can develop a mature political system. We have to change the way our voting system works, because it's not working. We have to look at the ways in which, from the top down, that structures, systems, have to be dismantled."

And there is a deep-seated frustration that the predicted benefits of the Good Friday Agreement are not being delivered – or, at least, not delivered for all of Northern Ireland society. Father Martin Magill observes: "There's a phrase that I've heard which I find very helpful. Not too far away from here [in West Belfast] is the Divis area. Within Divis there's a street called Albert Street, which has known a lot of trouble. It's had a lot of so-called joy riding and other anti-social behaviour. One of the phrases I hear is, 'Unless the people on Albert Street see the difference the peace process makes to their lives'. Unless we see this peace process start to address some of that and the Creggan or West Belfast or the Lower Newtownards Road, or parts of the Shankill. There's so many of those areas in the city [of Belfast] and throughout Northern Ireland where there's issues that have to be resolved - educational underachievement. Some really good youth projects, funding those projects, would be the first ways I would start."

Clare Bailey MLA, leader of the Green Party in Northern Ireland, makes a similar argument. "We've had a process over the past 20 years and we've called it 'a peace process'," she remarks. "We have to look at what has happened in those 20 years, because I'm of the firm opinion that we've had a political process at the cost of a peace process. We have to look at where have the benefits been in the past 20 years. Working class, the most deprived, areas in Northern Ireland and those communities, certainly haven't seen a pay-off."

Clare adds: "We have more peace walls in Northern Ireland now than we did during the conflict. Our education system hasn't moved on.... There's a huge amount to be done in trying to bring people together and

---

"We have more peace walls in Northern Ireland now than we did during the conflict."

---

let them work together. Obviously we can't knock down our housing stock and build this new way of living, but over the past 20 years I've seen little attempt at integration. The investment in the political process has been very burdensome. A lot of red tape, a lot of slow decision-making: the Assembly when it was up and going actually delivered very little. While it provided a space and a place to have debates, it hasn't gone hand-in-hand with true reconciliation and peace building."

Former UUP leader Mike Nesbitt, who remains an MLA, argues that to meet the needs of Northern Ireland society we need to change the way politicians approach their role and the way the electorate use their votes. He recalls: "What I found strange, when I made my pitch for the Ulster Unionists working with the SDLP and trying to go for a post-sectarian election, was that very few seemed to recognise that in our elections, unlike a general election where one party tends to go into 10 Downing Street, after an Assembly election two parties *must* go into Stormont Castle, the equivalent of Downing Street. One unionist, one nationalist. Why do unionists only express an opinion on which unionist party they want on the ground floor when they have a single transferable vote and could equally express an opinion about whether they would like the SDLP or Sinn Féin on the first floor? And equally nationalists by and large tend to only express an opinion about whether they want Sinn Féin or the SDLP. I think that's where we have to get to and to talk about it in political terms."

"Let's make Northern Ireland work."

He adds: "When Colum Eastwood took over the SDLP I heard him use a phrase that I had been using – 'Let's make Northern Ireland work'. When I talked to him we were using the same measurements - quality of the health service, education system, prosperity of our people. Not just on how many pounds in the back pockets and purses, although that's important, but also their sense of wellbeing. Everybody now recognises that Northern Ireland per head of population has one of the worst rates of poor mental health and wellbeing. If you set your political stall to try to fix all that and improve all that, that's a lifetime's work."

The challenge of working in partnership applies not only within Northern Ireland's politics, but also between the political systems of the north and the south. Fergus O'Dowd TD, Fine Gael's representative for Northern Ireland relationships, observes: "Everybody is entitled to their view. I believe in working with the unionist parties. I believe in co-operation. I believe in working with people to bring about change. I get on well with my colleagues in other parties. I meet occasionally with members of the British-Irish Inter-Parliamentary, so I've met some of the unionists, not too many of the DUP. I would like to engage more with the DUP because I need to understand their position better. I have met moderate unionists and I understand their position absolutely and respect it. I've met moderate nationalists.

"I just think we need to engage more in the south with the majority party in the north, which is the DUP, and obviously that's something that they don't want to do. I was chairman of the Fine Gael Brexit Group at one stage under our previous leader, Enda Kenny. I wrote to all the leaders in the Northern parliament and I met them all. The only people that wouldn't meet me were the DUP. I said, 'Why not?'. So I'll have a go again now and hopefully I'll do a bit better. We don't threaten anybody."

It seems it is time to move on to the next stage of the peace process, which must be regarded as still underway – and not a completed process. Asked if what we have at present is the absence of war without all the benefits of peace, Claire Sugden agrees.

Some MLAs believe the next stage of progress requires reform of the voting system within Stormont. Since the interviews were conducted, this has been partially achieved with the agreement to use petitions of concern only in the most unusual of circumstances, as a last resort. For Clare Bailey, a primary requirement is the end of sectarian designations for voting. "A discussion needs to be had in terms of updating or developing the Good Friday Agreement," she believes. "It was never meant to be a forever process. It was a 'for now' process, but yet we haven't evolved very much from there."

Clare explains: "We still have the same political discourse and rhetoric dominating. While it's valid to be nationalist or unionist, I think that sectarianism has been written into the very heart of our institutions. I have to designate myself as either a nationalist or a unionist. If I don't agree with either, or don't identify as either, I'm automatically discounted as 'other'. And what's 'other'? I designated myself as a feminist when I was first elected. The computer does not compute. So I am automatically an 'other'. So my 'other' vote in some Assembly debates is lesser than a nationalist or unionist. It's [in] those types of machinations that I mean by sectarianism being written into the heart of the institutions. How can that be fit for the future when our institutions are embedded within a sectarian notion?"

Bailey is one of several interviewees who believes the politicians in the main parties should have been guided towards long term solutions through the involvement of outsiders – reflecting the roles in the past of US special envoys to Northern Ireland, George Mitchell and Richard Haas. A similar role might have been taken from someone from another country, or perhaps someone with a non-party background. In practice, the former Secretary of State Julian Smith and former Tánaiste Simon Coveney undertook a similar role to bring about the restoration of the Assembly and Executive.

"I'm not claiming to have all the answers, but proper civic involvement could be managed by an outsider," Bailey suggests. "What we've got now is a very staid politics and political leadership. We know where they're coming from and they're not moving on and when it comes to election time we just need to scratch the surface and get people out voting on identity. While they can still do that, something else has to happen in the background. We need a dual process where wider civic society have that engagement and the proper full engagement. I believe that can be managed by an outside independent arbitrator."

John McKinney – a former head of the SEUPB in Northern Ireland and now an international peace negotiator – has mixed feelings about the use of outsider intermediaries. He says brokers have been helpful in bringing peace in other countries "a little, but not as much as people would think." John reflects on how other countries with internal conflicts – such as Cyprus and Columbia – address their difficulties. He explains: "They might have maybe a key mentor as it were, maybe from South Africa or someone from the USA or someone from Northern Ireland."

John says the process begins with "getting local buy-in where people see that they want to get involved. Then they can see the benefit of getting involved." Information is then provided to key people on a managed basis to improve confidence, encouraging greater involvement and seriousness. This process is assisted by the external broker. In a society like Northern Ireland, which is a well-developed society, I don't think we really need to do that.... What we need to have is a vision of the top, we need to have support for that vision, we need faith in that vision, and we need to feel as if we're being wanted to be part of that."

One approach, John adds, might be for the Assembly to continue to function, even if again in future the Executive again does not. If the Assembly were to meet even if the Executive does not it might assist with relationship building at the level of individual MLAs, providing opportunities for the MLAs to meet and talk outside of formal structures – for example, in the Stormont cafes.

There is a wide selection of opinions on how to make progress. Most importantly this demonstrates that ideas are there on how to avoid political stagnation and to cement the peace process by doing things differently and in a spirit of partnership. Those opinions need to be considered with regard to political leadership, just as they do with regard to a range of other difficult challenges as we shall recount in the following chapters.

CHAPTER TWO
TRUTH & RECONCILIATION

"We cannot deal with things, if we don't talk about them."
Mihaela Bernard, psychoanalyst.[1]

It is an accepted principle within psychoanalysis that to recover from trauma, it is necessary to identify the causes and reflect on them. Yet as a society, Northern Ireland has adopted the opposite approach – to try to ignore much of the past hurt as if that will enable society to move on. Many members of society, in the north and the south, believe that is the wrong attitude. It means our progress is held back.

Obviously there is fear that talking about the causes of, and the actions in, the Troubles could reignite anger and violence. There is also a case to be made that one of the main reasons for not dealing with the past is that the truth of the past is so embarrassing and damaging. The Troubles were a dirty conflict, where wrong things were done by people on all sides.

Ireland Senator Mark Daly – formerly chair of the Oireachtas Good Friday Implementation Committee and currently Cathaoirleach of Seanad Éireann – observes: "The problem with the politics is that there are so many people who have so much to hide on all sides, on the paramilitary sides and the police in the north, in the south, in Britain, the system and the establishment, in every way, shape or form, on unionist and loyalist sides, republicans and nationalist sides.

"There are so many people who have so much to hide on all sides."

"The paramilitaries have a lot to hide because they had informers in their own ranks and people in some instances don't want that coming out and politically that can be damaging from their own point [of view]. Same with Britain, what they were up to; the Irish government in terms of the stuff that they did and didn't do during the Troubles. So the system is quite happy to hide all the stuff that it has hidden for so long because it doesn't want that information coming out, but then the consequences are for the citizens and civilians who continue to seek justice."

The question is whether Northern Ireland can learn from best practice elsewhere – and, if so, where that best practice has taken place. Lord Robin Eames – formerly Archbishop Eames of the Church of Ireland and co-chair

---

1 Mihaela Bernard is a psychoanalyst and author. Similar views are held across the psychoanalytic profession.

of the Consultative Group on the Past in Northern Ireland – says: "I had a lot of conversations with Desmond Tutu in South Africa over the Truth and Reconciliation Tribunal that was happening in Cape Town. And the more I listened to him and the more we compared notes, the more I'm convinced that the real elephant [in the room] in looking at the past is honesty.

"Not honesty that would suit my party, my community, but honesty at a level where society has moved to say, 'Yes, that happened. Yes, someone in my community caused it.'. But the truth is that has to be ticked off as part of the history and you want a totally independent body looking at that in terms of this is what happened and this is where we move on. That's not to say you put a camouflage over it. It's not to say you say, 'Oh, that's irrelevant, that's in the past.'. You should face up to it and you say 'Hurtful, dangerous though it is, this is what happened. This is why we caused it all. We had a role in it. Let's put it on the table and let's move on'."

Robin adds that it is important to act quickly, while actors (and victims) of the Troubles are still alive. He explains: "People that I worked with over the years during the Troubles, people who had a key role in how things unfolded, some of them are gone. They can't speak from the grave. We've got records of what they did, we have opinions of what they did and we've got comments by those who worked with them. But their voice is lost because history has moved on."

Mike Nesbitt draws on his experience as a victims' commissioner, as well as being an MLA and former leader of the Ulster Unionist Party. He believes that we are glossing over the past and its impact on people. Mike explains: "As a victims' commissioner I spoke to a lot of people. Victims are not an homogeneous group of people, but there are common experiences. The one that first hit me, and hit me very hard, was that you might think that if something catastrophic happened to you, that you were injured or you lost your partner, your loved one was killed, that the first thing that would happen is the state would form the wagons in a circle. So if you needed medical help, the health service was there for you. If you needed your children taken to school, the education system was there for you. If you needed money....

"The common experience was you were ignored and forgotten. So then if you look at a comprehensive assessment of the needs of victims you will find that truth and justice is not even on the podium, it's not in the top three. At the top are mental health and wellbeing. I accept that some people's poor mental health and wellbeing is directly attributable to the fact they haven't had truth and justice, so we've got concentric circles going on here. But if we tackled mental health and wellbeing in a very serious way we would help an awful lot of victims to get to a better place. And maybe a place where they are reconciled to what has happened to them. And the commonality of the experience of receiving poor mental health and wellbeing because of a catastrophic act that happened to them. The commonality of that fact, irrespective of why it happened or who was responsible for it happening, may actually help us move forward."

He adds: "Politicians need to learn to listen harder to victims and what they need. They may conclude that sometimes what victims want is not in their best interests. For example, if you have a vulnerable victim who is prone to taking too much alcohol, giving them a big lump sum of money may not be in their best interests, even if that's what they say they want. There is a disconnect between what victims want and what society wants."

The truth is that while the pain and trauma persist, any comprehensive approach to a judicial process of justice is now impossible to achieve. Peter Sheridan argues: "There has to be an honesty. That honesty is that we will never do justice to the scale of the injustice on any side. If I take the simplest of issues - somebody going to put a bomb under my car, 30 years ago. Is justice for me the person who's putting the bomb under the car? Is justice for me the person who made the bomb? Is justice for me the person who hijacked the car, took the house over? Or is it the person at the very top of the tree, who authorised it? Or indeed is justice for me the person who was sitting in the chapel on a Sunday, instead of saying their prayers was taking notes and passing information on about my movements?

"The reality is you're never going to get to all of those, even if you got to one of them. My experience in court is that once victims hear the full story they will naturally want to know, 'Who was it in the chapel? I would like to see the colour of their eyes.' I think politicians have to be clear to everybody out there, we are not going to reach a stage of utopia where this will be justice for everybody and in every case and every aspect of it."

Even where judicial action can proceed, the impact can be very negative on victims and survivors. Peter recalls: "I sat in a legacy case where a police officer had been shot dead and he was 23 years of age. His wife was in hospital. She got remarried. But 35 years later they discover a piece of forensic evidence that actually leads to the person being brought to court. In court, the individual was convicted, but under the Good Friday Agreement the maximum they get is two years in jail. So the first question, how does that feel in terms of justice?

"But worse than that, she [the widow] learned things in court for the first time. She understood her husband had died right away. Turns out, he was alive for a number of minutes and he called her name during that last four or five minutes of his life. That's the first time she learned that. We just re-traumatised the individual and the notion that because that person was in court, and all of the complexity for his family as well, I don't think we did justice anywhere in the wider sense of what we mean by justice. I fear that that narrow view of justice of somebody being in court convicted and going to jail is not going to deliver what we think is justice."

A similar point is made by solicitor Philip Gilliland – a business leader who is a former president of the Londonderry Chamber of Commerce. He observes: "I'm not a criminal lawyer so I can't answer directly about the technicalities, but my sense of the administration of justice and the past is that it's just so vast and so difficult a task to apply legal justice to events of over 20 years ago, that it's just not practical. You've got how many unsolved murders and then multiply that by a factor of probably 20 or 30 or more for other unsolved acts of violence. Many of the witnesses are dead, and many of the witnesses who are still alive with the passage of time their memories may be playing tricks on them. They may not even remember what they think they remember, etc. What is the truth?

"With a very heavy heart I can't see us going back to the administration of justice in the technical sense, in the juridical sense, to deal with the past. All of us over the age of probably 45 have to a lesser or greater degree suffered some degree of trauma as a result of violence. Obviously some people suffered vast trauma and others only very mild peripheral trauma, but we're all a part of it. I would say a healthy majority of people over the age of 45 carry with them some degree of trauma about the past.

"You know, very, very few people who got involved in a paramilitary activity or violence perpetrated by the state, were what you might call a sociopath. 99% of people who got involved, for whatever reason, believed

---

"99% of people who got involved, for whatever reason,
believed they were doing the right thing."

---

they were doing the right thing. A part of that was the dehumanisation of the person who was going to be your victim. Now that we're talking to each other again, it must be quite challenging for the perpetrator to find a humanised person associated with their victim. When the perpetrator goes home and they say, 'Goodness me, and I did that to his brother. Why did I do it?'. There's a tremendous toll on their own mental health and an awful lot of this is in the territory of mental health support. We are quite a damaged society, particularly for people over the age of 45 and I am told there are intra family consequences for the next generation which may or may not explain one of the reasons why we have such a high suicide rate amongst young people. Is there some connection there? I don't know."

Philip adds: "Given that the administration of justice in the technical sense is probably not going to deliver the answers, certainly not going to deliver a lot of the truth, what actually is required in my view, if it were possible, is a policy of truth. Why don't the forces of the state, the government, why don't Sinn Féin or the IRA, why don't the loyalist paramilitaries and politicians, why don't they tell us what happened? I can think of loads of people who were killed and nobody has a clue who killed them and why they were killed. Well somebody knows. It's far, far too late for the people who pulled the trigger and the people who ordered them to pull the triggers, it's too late for them to go to jail. Jail is not the point. But what would be extremely good for the healing process is to know, 'Well, why did you pull the trigger? What was it in you that said that was a good idea? And were you just following orders? Why did you follow orders? And the person that gave you the order, why did you give the orders? Why did you think that was a good idea?'."

Sophie Long, formerly a candidate with the Progressive Unionist Party and now a worker with a charity seeking to improve Northern Ireland, makes a series of interesting observations about the continuing impact of the Troubles in terms of inter-generational trauma and how our society works – and often doesn't work very well – today.

"Most people here, either inter-generationally or directly, understand the conflict in a way that means they ascribe," says Sophie. "There are a set of people who either don't want to talk about the conflict or understand the nature of ethnic conflict and understand that there are different forces at play. But then there are big, big chunks of people who think, 'Look, my family suffered', or 'My family were in the security services and we didn't want this to happen to us'. And no matter what the other arguments are, they can't bear the idea of somebody that visited harm on them enjoying political power. They're hearing stories passed down and it resonated with them and then it's much more difficult to get people to vote in cross-sectarian ways."

What is happening, suggests Sophie, is that politics today is being used to play out the past violence as a different type of conflict. She argues that the voting for politicians – and more specifically voting against another set of politicians - is "another form of struggle, it's another form of conflict because you want somebody else to lose out." She continues: "But the only reason we want somebody else to lose out is because you think they've done something bad to you, or that you can't trust them.

"And I've said this when I've been asked to speak at Sinn Féin oriented events. Some of the policies that Sinn Féin have are fine, I wouldn't mind them implementing them. Some of the people in the party are really dead on, really progressive, really good thinkers and I like them. But I still don't know if I would trust them, if this was going to be a unitary state and they were the largest political party, I don't know if I would feel comfortable. And nobody in the Provisional IRA or in Sinn Féin as the local party has ever done anything bad to me, but there's still that broad suspicion, that some of the offers they're making about representing Britishness in a new Ireland don't tally up with their behaviour in Northern Ireland as it is. And I fully understand people who are Irish or Irish nationalist or Irish Catholic wouldn't want to be in a state that was run by parties like the DUP because of the way they talk about those citizens. So some of the veto stuff is about trust, you're just thinking, 'What would you do to me if you were able to?'."

Indicating the lack of common trust in our society still present today, Sophie asks: "If you look at the attitudinal stuff: would you be comfortable living in the same community, or even the mad question, 'Would you trust somebody from the other community to hold a ladder for you?'. Those little things, they're all tied to memories of what they did and in the sense that they're not sorry. They might periodically act like they're sorry, they might give a sort of apology in that 'Sorry people were harmed', but not 'I am sorry that I did those things and I won't do it again.'.

"You could look at that from both sides. You could say the people who support Sinn Féin or some of the smaller republican parties, do they reject violence not just because it's not strategically useful, but they reject violence on moral grounds? And you could ask people from a unionist persuasion, 'Do you recognise the structural violence visited upon the Catholic population was wrong and can you explain why you recognise that?'. I suppose it's the same as in an intimate relationship with somebody who just says to you, 'I'm sorry'. You need to know why they're sorry, that they've actually reflected on what they've done and that they've made steps to change their behaviour, so they're not going to do it again, because we haven't really had any of that if you think about it."

For nationalists/republicans, and even for many unionists, the British state cannot be seen as a neutral party – they were involved in the Troubles as participants and the use of state agents remains a point of strong contention. This was revealed in the inquiry into collusion by Lord Stevens, during which investigators concluded that of 210 people they arrested, 207 were state agents.[2] "Suddenly they [the UK government] are not neutral actors trying to broker peace among two warring tribes," observes Sophie. "They were a very active part of a conflict that went on for far longer than it should have. So yes, the Stevens Inquiry was massive, the findings of it were under-recognised and yet the action that you would assume would be taken then hasn't been taken and there's a very inconsistent approach to all of those deaths."

Sophie is a strong supporter of the proposed Oral History Archive[3] to collect stories, emphasising that the definition of 'a victim' can be too narrow. "We need to remember that we tend to look into killings from a masculine position. We don't think thoroughly about gender and about the gendered impact of what went on. Sometimes people will say, "Okay so a man was killed and we don't know how he was killed, so we've got to find out what time he was killed and where was he, who else was in the house.". But they won't ask if his partner saw it, if his mum saw it, if they were pulled out of the way beforehand and all that kind of cumulative impact of that violence on women who might not have been killed, but who suffered for years and years and years."

At the heart of the tragedy of the Troubles is that extraordinary times led to people doing extraordinary things – often terrible extraordinary things. In the words of Sophie: "But you wouldn't know the madness, that if the Troubles hadn't kicked off here 90% of people in prison would never have went to prison. They would never have felt the urge to be violent towards anybody and then we probably wouldn't have all the mental health issues we have and all the prescription medication issues that we have."

"There was more to the Troubles than just Catholic and Protestant."

Perspective is important - and can be assisted by trying to consider the past with objectivity and open mindedness. Author and Museum of Free Derry staffer Julieann Campbell makes the point: "There was more to the Troubles than just Catholic and Protestant." Historian Anthony Russell expands that by saying:

2 https://www.irishtimes.com/culture/books/secrecy-and-northern-ireland-s-dirty-war-the-murder-of-pat-finucane-1.2796750
3 http://rightsni.org/2015/10/the-stormont-house-oral-history-archive-proni-and-the-meaning-of-independence-guest-post-by-dr-anna-bryson/

"We have to recognise, and the voters have recognised it for us, that there are two ethnic communities here and we should not underestimate the power of ethnicity.... We'd be very foolish in the north of Ireland to ignore just how deep ethnicity is. We may not like it but any problems we have, have to be approached recognising that we have two very distinct communities here."

Anthony believes that an objective consideration of Irish history can help to overcome some of the prejudices associated with that ethnic identification. He explains: "From my Catholic perspective, approaching it to realise that our social democracy actually starts with King William and comes through the French Revolution, the American Revolution through to where we are at the moment. I would now trace our social democracy back to the Battle of the Boyne and realise probably the Catholics for ethnic reasons were on the wrong side at the Battle of the Boyne. James was a dictator and as we have seen, when you have a Catholic state, a la de Valera, sometimes it's not a very attractive place at all."

Moving forward, we need to reflect on the Troubles as a period of shared tragedy, in which the experience of people living in Northern Ireland was one to a large extent of commonality, not of difference. Julieann Campbell observes that her research led to her seeing things with a different perspective. "Some of the strongest work that I've done in recent years was with the security forces," she explains. "And I would naturally, being from my community, I would have been afraid to speak to those people, but they were some of the most powerful interviews I've ever done and it was really, really interesting to hear that point of view, because it was something that I had never, ever been privy to before....It just showed that the hurt and the fear were universal and that was very important. Even the reserve police officers on the streets, they had the same fear as the people on the streets and that's important to know all these years later."

Those interviews with former security personnel have changed Julieann as a person, she says. "It has affected me on several levels, emotionally and in my work. It has made me more sensitive. It has made me more empathetic towards people I meet and it has made me less judgemental. It has opened my eyes to the hurt that is still here that I would never have seen if I hadn't indulged in this kind of work. So it was a real eye opener for me personally."

If acknowledgement of past pain and wrongs is important, can this be assisted by a 'day of acknowledgement' or similar? Father Martin Magill refers to the proposal from the Reverend Harold Good for a day of acknowledgement. "That sense of having a day where we acknowledge the past. To some extent the Day of Reflection provides a bit of that, but it's a different type of day, where there's an acknowledgement of some of the things that we didn't do well or did badly. There's a real value in that as well as acknowledging the huge amount of suffering we caused and never wanting to go back to that."

Martin says that his experience of a cross-community, non-denominational event of remembrance provides an example of an activity that can help with healing. He was involved with the Reverend Chris Hudson - a non-subscribing Presbyterian, the minister of All Souls Church in Belfast's Elmwood Avenue – in a "solemn reading, in alphabetical order, of every single name of anybody who was killed in the Troubles from 1969 onwards". He explains: "The focus we wanted to have was on people suffering, rather than going into the details of how this person died and was this person an innocent victim or a perpetrator, or whatever it is. We instead focused on the question of the loved ones left behind, irrespective of what he or she or they did, inevitably people would be left to suffer as a consequence of their death."

In reflecting on our shared past it is important to focus on how similar much of it was, particularly for those who lost love ones. Freya McClements, co-author of Children of the Troubles – which chronicles the lives and deaths of the children who died – observes: "It's the commonalities of human experience. That's where you build the connections." Former Church of Ireland Bishop of Derry Ken Good comments: "I think it was Mary McAleese who said that we have a shared history, but we don't have a shared memory. That's a powerful analysis. We don't have a shared memory yet."

Former health and finance minister Simon Hamilton wonders if Northern Ireland can learn from the Holocaust Memorial Day. While Irish language activist Linda Ervine suggests we consider the experience of Hiroshima, destroyed at the end of the Second World War by a nuclear bomb, and now dedicated to peace.

In both dealing with the past and the present, it is essential to 'humanise' the people around us, including those who have been permanently injured. The dehumanisation of people from a different community was important for many actors in the Troubles to behave as they did. One person who has been widely praised for his work in humanising people has been the artist Colin Davidson, who has portrayed some of those left disabled by events during the Troubles.

"Colin Davidson has done some remarkable work in terms of victims and survivors and one of the things that Colin says is that most of the people that he's worked with, what they're looking for is an acknowledgement of their suffering," says Councillor John Kyle of the Progressive Unionist Party.

"We have failed to acknowledge the suffering and loss adequately of the people who have lost and who have suffered."

"Now I personally did not lose anybody in the conflict. I knew people, I had friends, but I didn't have anyone close to me that I lost, so I realise that I have to tread warily here. But we have failed to acknowledge the suffering and loss adequately of the people who have lost and who have suffered.

"Secondly, we still struggle in terms of blame and recognition. Who is at fault, who is to blame and how we interpret the past and we've got different interpretations and those interpretations are often in conflict, and often painfully in conflict for the people who were involved. My understanding is that during the negotiations behind the Good Friday or Belfast Agreement that one of the first things George Mitchell did was to take the politicians out of the current situation here, take them away and enable them to relate to one another as human beings. And there's a huge need for us still to do that, to relate to one another as human beings, not as political opponents, or as the other side, or as the enemy, or as the cause of my suffering.

"We need to find new contexts to enable people to talk together. I know that there have been loads of very noble and very worthwhile initiatives in the past - Healing Through Remembering[4], the Wave organisation - but there is just an ongoing need for that and particularly for some of the people who have suffered the most and who perhaps have not received the support, the recognition, the help that they deserve and need. There needs to be a refocusing on that to help them and part of the difficulty of course, as we all know, is that where politicians differ and disagree then constituents, or the people in the community, suffer. And our politicians' failure to find some way forward in dealing with the past has exacerbated the suffering of victims and survivors."

Understanding the legacy of pain, disability and death is unpleasant, but it is necessary as a means of trying to avoid a return to violence. We have peace, but it is not certain that it is permanent. Senator Mark Daly commissioned Professor Pat Dolan, Professor Mark Brennan and former US national security advisor Michael Ortiz to consider the risks of a return to violence

---

4 https://healingthroughremembering.org/

in Northern Ireland[5]. Mark Daly observes that only a minority of adults were involved in violence during the Troubles, and again only a minority of adults and teens are at risk of becoming involved in violence now – but that it only takes a small number of people to create a very big problem.

Mark argues that it is important to remove the romanticism from the story of the Troubles, as a warning to a new generation not to engage in conflict. "History could be used as a tool against itself and what they [Dolan, Brennan and Ortiz] term as instead of using history as a way of mobilising communities to settle grievances from the past," he says. "And as we all know, even God can't change the past so trying to settle grievances by using force is not the way forward. But what they do is they talk about using history as a way of teaching people the consequences of violent resistance and the consequences for ordinary people." Mark adds that still today, it can be a local paramilitary leader who has status and a form of respect in his community.

Simon Hamilton warns that the past remains extremely difficult. "The past is a subject we're struggling with," he concedes. "It's wrong to call it the past, because it's part of the present and it will be part of our future as well. How we teach it is incredibly sensitive. I know from talking to school groups in my own constituency [he was an MLA for Strangford] and the ones that come to Stormont from time-to-time that they are taught about Northern Ireland politics and it tends to be post '98 and how we came together, but there's very little about [the past] – and you can understand why teachers are reluctant to get into it without a lot of support and guidance. It can't be done on an ad hoc basis, there needs to be a very clear structure to that sort of a process."

Andrew McCracken, chief executive of The Community Foundation for Northern Ireland, warns that while government in Northern Ireland has been a 'zero sum game' fought over between representatives of the two main traditions, the telling of the story of the past is similar. There is no common narrative of what happened or why. The reality is that "Nobody has clean hands", in the words of Mike Nesbitt. Linda Ervine agrees, saying: "Those who cheered on share responsibility for what happened."

Peter Sheridan has argued that the Northern Ireland Executive should establish a 'Department for Reconciliation', with responsibility for bringing our society together. Mark Daly responds that if this were to happen, it is essential that it is properly resourced. The Alliance Party has a different

---

5 Northern Ireland Returning to Violence as a Result of a Hard Border due to Brexit or a Rushed Border Poll

approach, but with the same objective. Its leader Naomi Long says: "We have proposed having what we have called 'PASS' as a sort of 'Policy Appraisal for Sharing over Separation', to look at every policy that's going through government and ask "What will the impact of this be?", and if it's going to enhance segregation, then what is the mitigation we're going to put in place to balance that out?"

Avila Kilmurray argues that to improve community relationships, two pre-conditions need to be met: to consider the lessons of the past and to read (or re-read) the Good Friday Agreement, to comply with the framework it sets out. She explains: "There was an inability and unwillingness to deal with the civil war from 1920, '21, '22, and the whole [southern] political system has been artificially formatted on those civil war alignments, which has distorted social and economic policies. I worry that is replicated in Northern Ireland. Unless we can talk about what happened - albeit there will be a kaleidoscope of experiences, a Protestant border farmer in west Fermanagh is totally different from a Catholic unemployed person in Ardoyne during the Troubles. But we need to create the space for those stories to be shared.

"We need to look at what happened in terms of the actual kills, with both the state and paramilitary organisations, loyalist and republican. Whether we will get to the truth as we move further away from the time period is more of an open question. Even if we got to the stage about individuals being held to account, as the intent was in South Africa, even if there was a degree of explanation from organisations about why they did certain things, for example, the IRA, their economic war and their targeting of contractors involved in building police stations as collaborators; the dirty war from the British government; to what extent there was collusion. That is the sort of thing there needs to be an open discussion around, otherwise history will be repeated."

Avila adds: "I've always argued - particularly working with people from other conflict societies like Cyprus, Sri Lanka - that the genius of the Good Friday Agreement was disentangling national aspiration, national identity, citizenship, because that provided the room for both identities. If that became unpicked - like over the whole Brexit issue - then it does raise issues about the basis whereby people voted in the referenda. We also then have the issue that the DUP campaigned against the referenda, they were soundly beaten, but very often they will say their premise is the St Andrew's Agreement, rather than the Good Friday Agreement. But the Good Friday/Belfast Agreement was massively supported. There was an ambiguity around it - not so much on citizenship, because it was very much you can be an Irish or British citizen and both, so that really shouldn't be unpicked. The ambiguity was around how to deal with the legacy of the past and those issues."

Father Martin Magill stresses: "Part of my DNA is to be neighbourly, friendly with those of other denominations. I could mention Alan McBride and his campaign of the good neighbours. I can't stress that enough." Martin believes that cross-community engagement between the faiths is an important element in this. The same point is made by the former Bishop of Derry, Ken Good, who talks of his close friendship with the Catholic Bishop of Derry, Donal McKeown. Much of making progress is about building relationships – a problem when our politicians of different traditions avoid social contact with each other.

CHAPTER THREE
RE-BUILDING CIVIC SOCIETY

"The current mechanisms for democracy that we have aren't all the tools that we need." Andrew McCracken, CFNI

It is often argued that civic society represents one of the strands of a truly democratic system. To put it another way, a clear indicator of an undemocratic authoritarian state is the absence of civic society.[6] An active civic society is a sign of freedom of expression and an ability to influence government in ways that go beyond the occasional or regular exercise of a vote. So it should be a matter of concern when a jurisdiction does not have an active civic society, or else one that is not influential. Many observers are concerned at the lack of influence of civic society within Northern Ireland.

Lord Eames talks of his preference for a 'People's Assembly' as a counter-balance to Stormont. He is also known as Robin Eames, who was the Church of Ireland Archbishop of Armagh and co-chair of the Eames-Bradley Commission, properly called the Consultative Committee on the Past. He likes the term 'People's Assembly' rather than 'Citizens' Assembly'. He explains: "We need to do a lot more research into the 'People's Assembly'

"People that talk to me have a tremendous degree of frustration for the lack of representation and understanding in the media of what really concerns them in everyday life."

---

concept. We need to do a lot more in how the media reflects what people on the ground are saying. The people that talk to me have a tremendous degree of frustration for the lack of representation and understanding in the media of what really concerns them in everyday life."

Asked why he uses the term a 'People's Assembly', he says: "It's very similar. That happens to be just the title that I find comfortable. And the structure is probably more important even than those who take part in it."

Citizens' assemblies have been very influential in the Republic of Ireland, bringing together a representative sample of the general population to consider in detail difficult policy challenges. In the south they considered

6 https://www.weforum.org/agenda/2018/04/what-is-civil-society/

same sex marriage and abortion – leading to significant constitutional reform – and also climate change. In France, a citizens' convention has advised the government on the policies needed to mitigate damage to the climate.[7]

While it has gained less attention than the Citizens' Assembly in the south, there is already experience of a citizens' assembly in Northern Ireland. This was run by the Community Foundation for Northern Ireland, led by Andrew McCracken, with additional funding brought in from elsewhere, focusing on social care and healthcare for the elderly.[8]

Andrew says: "If we want to transform civic society, the current mechanisms for democracy that we have aren't all the tools that we need and that's true across the UK. We funded Northern Ireland's first independent citizens' assembly in November [2018], where you get 80 people who are demographically representative of all of Northern Ireland and invite them to take two weekends to be briefed by experts and debate policy issues and recommendations on that policy issue. We were overwhelmed by the response, so we used a polling company to help us get our 80 people and make sure they were representative. The polling company wrote to 4,000 people. Within two days, we had 300 volunteers, people saying, 'Yes, I'll set aside two weekends of my time to do this'.

"It was a debate about healthcare. We're all getting older and there's not enough money to look after us. So these were really tricky things that we're wrestling with. We were able to have a meaningful conversation and come up with some recommendations together. And it was bloody hard work: it wasn't easy, but we did it. For me there's a transformation of civic society there that's giving people the confidence that we're able to participate and make decisions together in a way that isn't about fighting the old political battles."

While citizens' assemblies can be of enormous value in providing an additional dimension in policy debate, they might be regarded as different to civic society – which tends to comprise the voluntary sector, charities, religious groups and special interest associations. Citizens' assemblies should be more representative of the population as a whole – providing they are convened carefully – but their promotion is not necessarily at the expense of civic society.

Difficult questions persist around the definition of 'civic society', how it can be comprised in ways that are in some sense democratic or representative and how it can be made accountable. But, argues Peter Osborne, there is a

7 https://europeanclimate.org/a-tale-of-two-citizens-assemblies/
8 https://citizensassemblyni.org/

strong record of civic engagement unlocking difficult challenges. Osborne is a former chair of the Parades Commission as well as having been chair of the Community Relations Council, giving him a perspective on past events that is worth close consideration.

Peter observes: "It's really important we find a mechanism for civil society to have its voice heard. If you looked at some of the issues that are problematic in politics in Northern Ireland today, I suspect if you handed some of those issues over to civil society they'd find an answer very quickly. Some people would say that's an argument for bringing back the Civic Forum, which was part of the Good Friday Agreement. I'm not overly in favour of bringing back a Civic Forum in that way. I think there were limitations to that. Part of the limitation in a practical sense was around the commitment to it by government, but also the funding it received. But also who was *on* that Civic Forum was a real issue and would continue to be a real issue.

"I am a fan of things like citizens' assemblies that we've seen working in the Republic of Ireland very, very successfully. And I was down at the Citizens' Assembly that dealt with the environment and what I saw there was a hundred people drawn from civil society, randomly sampled, geographically spread, different genders, different age ranges, different socio-economic backgrounds, no political baggage. And they were *really* intensely exploring issues from the perspective of the evidence, not from the perspective of anything around political politics or around what constituency they would have to represent or who might have more influence on who gives them votes. And they explored the evidence and they came up with conclusions that were just logical that therefore would be good policy based on good evidence.

"And when you look at the two big successes of the Citizens' Assembly in the south around same sex marriage and reproductive rights, you have essentially politicians devolving, making recommendations to a Citizens' Assembly who look at the evidence, come up with recommendations, and then it's endorsed at a referendum. And in those two cases, you had change on major social issues that caused the political parties difficulty, but the process itself allowed the political parties to engage in a process where they weren't then taking decisions. They were allowing the Citizens' Assembly to look at options based on evidence and then [for] people in the whole country to take the decision at the end of the day.

"So there are mechanisms that work. In Northern Ireland we need to find mechanisms to allow civil society to have the voice. When you look at some

"It's really important we find a mechanism for civil society to have its voice heard."

of the big successes of the peace process over the last 20 years, two of the big successes, I would argue, are policing and parading. What do they have in common? When policing reform was mooted and then processed, you had a panel from civil society led by Chris Patten, with people from Northern Ireland who came up with that report and shaped policing and the change in policing. I think anybody from any political party or any political persuasion would say that has been a big success. Confidence in policing has increased substantially, albeit there are still challenges.

"On parading, you had a Parades Commission that was established *from civil society*. You had seven people drawn from across the community. I chaired it for a number of years and was a member of it for a number of years. In the nine years that I was involved in the Parades Commission we never took a single vote. It was based on discussion and consensus of people coming from across the community and while we didn't get everything right, we got most things right in a really contentious, sensitive area of peace building here around parades. Civil society coming together, they can take decisions and they can take good decisions.

"We cannot afford another 10 or 20 years of focusing exclusively on political institutions as the way forward for this peace process."

"Part of this is about understanding that when you build peace here, and we're less than halfway through our peace process, it is about relationships and that is about relationships within civil society. That leads to all sorts of issues around structural change, but it also means that we cannot afford another 10 or 20 years of focusing exclusively on political institutions as the way forward for this peace process. Yes, they're important, but it's relationship building that is at the heart of peace building."

There is an interesting suggestion that perhaps the best use for citizens' assemblies in Northern Ireland would not be to replicate their use in the south, but rather focus on more localised issues. Civic engagement was key to resolving very contentious and damaging parading issues in Derry-Londonderry, leading to a broadly satisfactory outcome. Perhaps this localised approach for civic engagement could deal with other difficult challenges.

Maeve McLaughlin – manager of the Conflict Transformation Peacebuilding Project, also called 'The Derry Model' and a former Sinn

Féin MLA – explains how parading disputes were resolved in the city. "We couldn't say the Derry Model equals this set of circumstances or experience. It's a mixture. It's our demographics. We had leadership, we had people who were willing to take risks. We have experiences: I wouldn't be naive enough to say we can simply lift those experiences and tailor them into other areas. But we have templates, we have a sense of people who were willing to take risks. That is a big important message for all our communities. It's how we use those experiences to cascade that learning to other places.

"In terms of parading, one of the big pieces coming out of engagement we're doing in Derry is the relationship that the Apprentice Boys have in the city with the residents' groups. The relationship that we have here in the Museum of Free Derry[9] with the Siege Museum[10] is unique. Also, in the city was the role of the business community and the fact that elements of the business community played a very proactive role in trying to reach an accommodation. The reality is that's not going to simply translate to other areas because, frankly, if it doesn't impact on a business and doesn't hit a business person in their pocket, they will not want to be dragged to the table to negotiate these things. But we have experiences, we have templates. If we think about the parading issue, even the process of developing what some people will call an accommodation, some people will call an agreement, it was a process where even down to the wording that was used other areas can learn by.

"The whole debate about when you have rights you have responsibilities was a big lesson in the city and again, as somebody who would have been very involved with the residents' group locally, that was a challenge for all sorts of people in all sorts of different communities. If you think about the debate around The Diamond [in the centre of Derry] and marching round The Diamond. The Diamond should be perceived as your city centre and a neutral place to be. What Derry was able to do at that stage was say, 'You're entitled to have your commemoration, but you also need to look at the rights and responsibilities.'"

> "When you have rights, you have responsibilities."

Peter Sheridan – chief executive of Co-operation Ireland and former assistant chief constable at the PSNI and RUC – believes that local citizens' assemblies should be used as a model to resolve other local disputes. He

---

9 The Museum of Free Derry tells the stories of Bloody Sunday, the Battle of the Bogside and Operation Motorman and is located in Derry's Bogside.
10 The Siege Museum tells the story of the siege of Derry and is located in the premises of the Apprentice Boys of Derry, in the centre of Londonderry.

argues: "There are a lot of good organisations who have come through the conflict and a lot of good community groups that are on the ground.... How do we get round the existing groups, involve new people and new ideas? There are models out there. Some of the work I'm looking at [is] in relation to building community capacity as part of the Fresh Start Agreement[11]. One [citizens' assembly] happened in the Republic of Ireland around the abortion debate. It works in Canada, it works in Iceland.

"There are examples all around the world: you pick an area and pick a problem, randomly select a group of people from the electoral register, and that could be depending on the size of the problem, it could be 30, 40, 50, 60 people, and you determine the size of the area. So it could be the size of the Creggan estate, or the west bank of the Foyle. You identify a particular problem. Let's take as an example that it may be how do we stop young people joining paramilitarism in area X? You randomly select 30, 40, 50 people, maybe even 100 people. You bring in expert opinion, for example, in Colombia here's how they went about stopping young people joining groups, in Spain this is how they stopped young people... and so on. And that randomly selected group ask the experts questions. Then they need time to deliberate and debate among themselves, properly facilitated, but also properly written up. That could be over a period of two weekends, two days, each weekend: that group would really engage in the conversation. And they would be remunerated for being present. So it's not a case of select people and you expect them to give up their time. If we value people's time and we value people from the civic society's time, then we should remunerate them for it.

"Once that conclusion or report is agreed then it goes into hopefully changed policy in the Executive and that would be the question as to where the policy-makers see it fitting and how they take it on board. Then that group is dissolved and then you start with a new problem and a brand new group randomly selected. And that way you exclude nobody because it could include political parties, it can include existing groups and existing organisations, it could include people who are in illegal organisations. But what you do get is you reach the two thousand people who turned out in east Belfast [after the murder of Ian Ogle]. You reach the five hundred people who turned out in Derry [after rioting], who desperately want to do something, want to make change, but are finding it difficult just to know how they make that change."

Peter believes that local citizens' assemblies could address a range of

---

11 The Fresh Start Agreement was reached between Northern Ireland's major parties in 2015 in an attempt to strengthen and stabilise the institutions of government.

issues affecting perhaps a deprived social housing estate, or bring together the two sides at an interface area. He explains: "It can be social issues, the very challenging issues of flags. I don't think there are any problems that are off limits. Some of the best thinking and ideas come from people who live in a community."

"Some of the best thinking and ideas come from
people who live in a community."

He adds: "This has to involve statutory agencies and to some extent all the statutory agencies. It could be an issue about education, health, but they have to engage in it and it is that disconnect that happens between statutory agencies and people on the ground because it doesn't necessarily get to all of the individuals who may have some of the best thinking. When I was in the police, some of the best ideas and thinking came out of officers who were on the ground, instead of people at the very top. It will require a thorough and genuine engagement by statutory agencies. But they shouldn't see it as a threat. This is meant to help and support, to improve a way of life for people in particular communities. It will be a challenge to statutory agencies."

If there is going to be local engagement between members of different communities, there needs to be a recognition of the commonality of the deprivation on both sides of many of the interfaces. Linda Ervine explains: "Peter Shirlow did a really good piece of research[12] looking at interface areas and I know this about the interface area that I come from myself. He said the major problem in these areas was not sectarianism. It was poverty, it was addiction, it was poor health, it was a lack of education, it was lack of opportunity. And unfortunately the area I come from became a dumping ground as well. So you would have a lot of people with a lot of problems and that's not going to be helpful. Interface areas need massive help.

"A lot of places in Northern Ireland have moved on and enjoy the dividends of peace. But if you're living in an interface area with a wall down the middle and still low level attacks, you didn't get that chance. They need extra help. There should be massive amounts of money and support poured in there. Their housing should be above average. They should have access to above average facilities. I also think, and this is very important, there should be youth work, work with the adults, that is only dealing with those areas.

12 A detailed social analysis of interface areas was conducted by E. Mark Cummings, Peter Shirlow, Brendan Browne, Clare Dwyer, Christine E. Merrilees and Laura K. Taylor.

Not the political representatives, not somebody that lives six streets away, people who are actually living in those particular streets and dealing with the aspects of having the wall or having stones coming over.

Linda adds: "It's very, very local level in things that need to be done. If the walls are going to come down and people are going to learn to live in peace with each other, then relationships have to be made first. You can't just take the wall down and say, 'Here you are, get on with it.'. There's a lot of intervention, a lot of money needs to be spent on skilling people. But if we have politicians coming in, or the community workers from six streets away, I don't think that's helpful. It is the actual people who are there, the actual neighbours, because that's what they are, neighbours."

Similar points are made by Father Martin Magill, who is a member of the Stop Attacks Forum. He recalls: "Let me go back to the [2018] Independent Reporting Commission[13] report. There was something very significant about some of its work, which focused on areas of social deprivation and paramilitary style attacks. There was such a correlation between the two. Whenever I'm talking about how we make sure young people don't get caught up with that, I want to look at it from a structural point of view, look at some of the deprivation and how we tackle that."

Frances Black – formerly a professional singer and now a member of the Irish Senate and a member of the Oireachtas Implementation of the Good Friday Agreement Committee – made two important observations about that committee's visit to the Falls Road and the Shankill Road. The social and economic conditions in the two neighbouring areas were very similar; and it was their social problems that were their priorities. "When I started to talk to them about mental health and the impact on young people, about what was going on, the deprivation, the lack of housing, the lack of jobs and all of those things, they started to come alive," she says. It is by focusing on those challenges that progress on bringing society together can be made, Frances suggests.

It is worth considering why the Civic Forum, an important element of the Good Friday Agreement, ceased to exist. Alan McBride, a victims' campaigner and a member of that Civic Forum, recalls: "It was a great idea. It had great potential. I don't think it was particularly well run or well managed. But I would like to see that idea come back and I would like our politicians not to see any form of Civic Forum or 'People's Parliament', call it what you will, as a threat to democracy. It's absolutely not. If politicians

---

13 First report of the Independent Reporting Commission

really tapped into it, it's an invaluable resource for them, even as a sounding board, to get some ideas, to have a proper interface with the community, with civil society. I think the first pilot Civic Forum in the early 2000s didn't achieve a lot, but not because of the people that were doing it. I just don't think it was particularly well chaired or well managed."

Mark Durkan – one of the architects of the GFA – believes it was not necessary for the Civic Forum to have been abandoned when the Assembly went down, nor was it right that it did end. "The Civic Forum became a casualty of suspension," says Mark. "There was nothing in the Agreement that said it should be a casualty of suspension. Some of us argued at the time that the Civic Forum should be maintained even though the Assembly was suspended. Then the North South Ministerial Council was deemed to be suspended as well and the north-south bodies were put into care and maintenance. And then some people felt well if that's happened to the north-south bodies then the Civic Forum should be parked as well. I believe that the Civic Forum was engaged in some good work."

What is more, argues Mark, the Civic Forum was preceded by engagement with civic society that was central to the success of the peace process. "We need to recognise that civil society made significant contributions during our peace process. Mo Mowlam as Secretary of State engaged civil society very strongly as a positive pressure point on the political parties. And we also were hearing from civil society through that period the benefits of partnership working, but already manifesting itself through the way in which EU funds were being used, often with quite innovative local delivery mechanisms and intermediary funding bodies that were bringing people together of very different backgrounds in new models of partnership in new ways and that were delivering things.

"There were practical lessons and experiences for people there that were reaching into politics, because some of those local partnerships involved local councillors, ex-prisoners, others, people who maybe wouldn't have been sitting in the same room or around the same table on other things. When we're talking about civil society we're not just talking about people who might be invited to an NIO reception or whatever, we're talking about people who are engaged in the here and now in their own neighbourhoods in everyday ways.

"When we negotiated the Agreement, one of the reasons we had a Civic Forum as part of the institutions was because we wanted to continue to harness that value and insight. I can remember talking about how a body like the Civic Forum could be used as outriders to cut through some of the challenging and structural policy issues that we would have to face, that maybe the formal government system of civil service papers and stilted stances from parties wouldn't cut through, not least on community relations, and some of the other issues that the Civic Forum could play a lead role on. We want to see not just the Civic Forum in the north, but also the consultative forum for north-south bodies as well.

"We thought that because civil society representatives, different sectoral voices, would come forward with authentic ideas for north-south cooperation, people wouldn't see this as north-south for its own sake, which was the kind of criticism that many unionists had of some of our ideas for north-south cooperation. So we were saying if your argument for north-south is that these have to be practical measures of mutual benefit and not an artifice for its own sake, well having this sort of level of civil engagement where you have the real sectoral players in there means that there will be credibility around some of these proposals and ideas, that they will be practical, so you don't have to worry that you're being sucked into some political agenda.

"There is a strong sense there that civil society has a voice that isn't always heard. We need to make sure that if we go forward with restoration of institutions, as I want to see, we need to make a priority of not just restoring the Civic Forum, but also looking to other mechanisms."

Despite that, it is clear that the two largest parties in Northern Ireland have serious concerns about the workings of the former Civic Forum and of any future replacement. Former finance, economy and health minister for the DUP, Simon Hamilton comments: "I don't like the phrase 'civil society'. I may not be alone within unionist ranks in not being comfortable with the phrase because of perhaps previous connotations - I think the first time I ever heard the phrase 'civil society' used was in and around the time of the Belfast Agreement. Obviously things were fairly charged and heated back then and a lot of unionists, particularly those who were anti-agreement at the time and probably still hold that position, would have seen civil society as something that would have been used against them to encourage them to accept a deal or an arrangement or an agreement that they didn't like. The old phrase 'the great and the good' is one often attributed.

"So we need to be careful in talking about civil society, that we're not just talking about the usual suspects - or maybe a new generation of usual suspects - who would be in that category of the great and the good, who would pop out from time to time to tell people what they were doing wrong and what they should be doing right in their opinion."

However, Simon recognises the possible value of a citizens' assembly in some limited instances. One might be where medical professionals and managers believe it is necessary to rationalise the health estate to improve outcomes and reduce waiting times which might involve, perhaps, closing a hospital, but there is public opposition to this and distrust of politicians in taking a decision. A citizens' assembly might, Simon concedes, be a route to gaining public acceptance of the need for significant public service reform.

For Sinn Féin, Máirtín Ó Muilleoir – another former MLA and finance minister - has concerns about who is represented in civil society debates, their legitimacy and their objectives. He explains: "Every voice has to be heard. There also have to be ground rules. You can't come in and talk at the table with everyone else but then go outside and be selling the drugs which are damaging the east Belfast community and then insist that I have to be at the table. So there are ground rules."

He adds: "I've seen in the past on different issues where business says, 'No, we only have regard to profit and the success of business'. And for me that isn't enough if you're saying, 'I speak for business, but I don't care about the dignity of people; I don't care about human rights; I don't care about where people get educated; or equal opportunity.'. So building civic society has to be more than saying, 'We're going to fund and make sure there are enough groups to speak for everyone', if people aren't willing to have a holistic view of whether it's business and it's people rather than profits. But if it's not inclusive for me that's not a strong civic society. I've seen that in the past, I've seen strong organisations from which I have been banned, even though I was an elected representative in Belfast, people saying, 'No, we won't let you through the door', but then they'd say, 'By the way, we're speaking for the greater good and speaking for all the people'."

By contrast, the former president of the Londonderry Chamber of Commerce, Philip Gilliland, argues that the coherence of the business organisations' response to Brexit does create a positive example for how civic society can be organised in the future. He says: "Thank goodness they [the business leaders] did get a clear run at the policy-makers and the Brexit negotiating team in London and a pretty clear run at the Brexit team in the south as well. They are reasonable, rational and speaking not just about their own members. They're speaking about the economic wellbeing of society going forward. It's a mandate to speak about the entirety of the futures for all of us in society."

This is especially true at times when there is an absence of political leadership, suggests Philip. "I feel that some business organisations are a very good vehicle for leadership in civic society. They allow people to emancipate themselves and say what they feel. My experience of being a business leader is that the audience that we were speaking to - which is not just businesses who are our members here in Derry, and not just the business community, the wider business community, but actually all of society - want to be led. They want leadership. They don't want spokespeople who remind everybody about all the old fears and bogeymen of the past. They want forward leadership."

There is an increasing view that it will need to be civic society rather than the political parties that lead on the discussion of the constitutional future of Northern Ireland. And that means the conversation needs to go far beyond groups that are dominated by individual political parties, genuinely engaging people from across society and traditions.

The former leader of the Ulster Unionist Party Mike Nesbitt explains: "Unionism needs to look and recognise that the environment around us is changing. The demographics are changing. That does not mean a united Ireland is inevitable, but it is something we need to be aware of. Scottish nationalism is a threat to the union, English nationalism is a threat to the union and I would go as far as to say that I believe the DUP and some of their policies, attitudes and tone is a long term threat to the union. So I would like to see civic unionism becoming more active.

"A few years ago with Peter Robinson I tried to activate them through the Unionist Forum. That was never going to work because although we got a lot of people in the room, some in the room were there to try and destroy the concept from the get go. So I look enviously at civic nationalism and their ability to come together in such big numbers at such short notice in the Waterfront Hall[14] and appear to emerge with a united front.

"So it's up to the politicians to give leadership here and try to energise people. We also need to learn that what we did in '98 was get power back from Westminster. But since then we have held it here on 'the hill' and it is long past time where we devolve the power off the hill into councils, through councils into communities, because the closer you get informed decision-making to the domestic unit, whatever that happens to be, the more the chance that you will facilitate positive change in people's lives."

One observation of concern made repeatedly by interviewees was the low voter turnout at elections and the disengagement of the electorate in

14 https://sluggerotoole.com/2019/01/20/beyond-brexit-waterfront-conference-to-focus-on-rights-and-the-future/

Northern Ireland politics. Father Martin Magill argues this is not to be confused with 'apathy', but rather with the sense that the current political system fails to deliver the results that voters want.

The scale of the problem is illustrated by the 2019 local government elections, where voter turnout in some council areas was below 50%, and the average across all councils was less than 53%[15]. Given that the Electoral Commission reports that around a quarter of eligible voters are not on the electoral register[16], that is a turnout of 53% of the 75% who are registered, or less than 40%. At the 2017 Assembly elections, turnout was 64.78%. After taking into account the one in four individuals not on the electoral register this equates to an election participation rate of just under 50%. This is poor by international standards[17], representing what might be considered a substantial democratic deficit.

Given the alienation of much of the population, we need to do politics in a different way, argues Northern Ireland Green Party leader, Clare Bailey MLA. She says: "We're stuck in this two party stalemate. The missing link is civic society. I think that the political process and the peace process have to be separate entities, because what we have at the minute is the notion that our political institutions can be so involved in the peace building mechanisms, for example, the Historical Inquiries Team, truth and reconciliation, oral histories.

"That needs to be removed and put firmly into the arena of civic society because this is a citizens' process, this is for wider society. The political involvement is way too much. I see an opportunity to roll-out a full, properly funded, resourced peace process and hand that to civic society to manage, while we learn what it is to be responsible politicians and learn how to do good governance."

It should be recognised, though, that there is more than one model by which civic society can be engaged in broadening democracy. Other options include community planning, participative budgeting and participatory democracy – each of which has advocates amongst our interviewees.

Carnegie UK has been promoting closer engagement by citizens in local service provision. Its trustee Aideen McGinley explains: "we're looking at

15 http://www.eoni.org.uk/Elections/Election-results-and-statistics/Election-results-and-statistics-2003-onwards/Elections-2019
16 https://www.electoralcommission.org.uk/who-we-are-and-what-we-do/our-views-and-research/our-research/accuracy-and-completeness-electoral-registers/2019-report-2018-electoral-registers-northern-ireland/completeness-northern-ireland
17 https://www.pewresearch.org/fact-tank/2018/05/21/u-s-voter-turnout-trails-most-developed-countries/

co-production, so that it is about working with people to determine what the plans will be and we're talking about shared leadership... people working together to prioritise, to get their plans, to articulate what's important to them locally and it's unique to each area".

Maureen Hetherington makes a similar point. "In any society we need a top down and a bottom up approach. Unfortunately not having anything at the top at the moment [while the Assembly was suspended], it relies very heavily on the bottom up approach. The citizens' assembly is a very good idea and it's very good to have people having a civil, mature conversation that draws out the common sense and the conclusions. You can reach a consensus and then you realise everything is about compromise."

For Father Martin Magill, one solution may lie in participatory budgeting, where local spending priorities are determined by the local community, working together. "That's the direction I'm going in. It could be a very useful way of helping us come together as a larger group, as a community. As people who live in an area, we know the issues best of all," he says. The group would determine "how money is spent in certain areas, there could be a real value in hearing local people give some sense of how they would like to see some of the spending."

Avila Kilmurray is critical of those politicians who see processes of public engagement as a threat. "It was really because there was no understanding that participative democracy doesn't replace representative democracy, it can add an element to it," she says.

CHAPTER FOUR
BRINGING SOCIETY TOGETHER

"We were all a bit naive in thinking that this was just a generational problem." Simon Hamilton

Time is said to be a healer, but at present the signs are that time of itself is not bringing Northern Ireland society together. Social divisions are, to a large extent, continuing down the generations, as are the attitudes that continue to divide different parts of our community.

"I think we were all a bit naive in thinking that this was just a generational problem," comments Simon Hamilton. "As people who lived through it and experienced it and perhaps were victims or survivors themselves got older and passed away, [it was assumed] that the problem would pass away almost with them. And it hasn't and it is being passed down and there's lots of science around how this gets passed on, even just through the behaviour of people - the struggles, the difficulties that victims went through particularly with their mental health and maybe sometimes their addiction and how they behaved and how that then gets passed on down through generations, but also just the interpretation of it. There is now a romanticism around it."

What perhaps exacerbates this is that the latest generation of political leaders now believes they have a legacy of obligation and guilt on behalf of their parents' and grandparents' generations not to 'sell out' their forebears. Simon agrees: "That's exactly right and also younger people coming through political ranks. And again, I bet you've said it, I've certainly said it, we just need a new generation coming through and it'll all be fine. And that's been shown to be the opposite actually in the case with many... I'm not trying to put everybody in the same basket, but there's a sort of, 'I have to prove myself that I am as tough as nails and I am not going to betray the cause'.

"I listen to some of it and I feel myself as an old man nearly in the Assembly now[18]. We used to be young once and a younger generation has come through. Of course, people might expect me to pick on Sinn Féin and there will be other younger ones in my own party's ranks and other parties too, but some of what is being said couldn't be from first hand. It's not from personal experience."

---

18 The interview was recorded before Simon stepped down as an MLA.

Simon explains: "There are some newer members whose families were involved or were victims themselves of the Troubles, so there is an understanding there. There's others who clearly haven't had that and it just becomes rhetoric, it's just a regurgitation of what they've heard through the years and there's not the authenticity to it. When I was first in the Assembly and was looking across at people who were in Sinn Féin but had a past in the IRA –and some of them said stuff that was offensive or hurtful or completely diametrically opposed to my viewpoint – but there was always a sense of 'We're not going back. We don't want to have that. We've gone through all of that but we're not going to have another generation go through it.'.

"And I'm not saying that some of these younger representatives are saying, 'We'll go back'. The tone is different because the experience is different. There is a danger. What I suppose I'm saying is that we can't just take for granted that because they didn't go through the Troubles that some of their rhetoric that perhaps led to the Troubles and would certainly have inflamed the Troubles during the 30 or so years of conflict isn't there again. I'm not saying that we'll fall back into violence or anything as a result of it, but it's not solving itself as generations move through."

To adopt a more positive focus, there are certainly projects that are excellent in bringing society together. But there is a serious question about whether they are sufficient. Peter Sheridan suggests the creation of a government department – the Department for Reconciliation – and Naomi Long proposes that all spending decisions are evaluated against the objective of social integration.

Senator Mark Daly is another with concerns. He says: "A lot of the great programmes are there, they'd been done and they are being done of a cross-community basis, but simply not on the scale that is required with the amount of money that is needed". Mark commissioned a report from

Professor Pat Dolan, Professor Mark Brennan and President Obama's security advisor Michael Ortiz (see chapter two) on how to prevent the radicalisation of future generations of young people in Northern Ireland. They concluded that much more needs to be done to address deprivation, to avoid their discontent being exploited by paramilitary leaders, "either in the use of republicans to achieve their aims of a border poll on a united Ireland, but then on the other side, loyalist paramilitaries wanting to maintain the status quo". Mark argues "what it needs is a scaled-up approach".

While much of the report argues for the need to tackle deprivation, it also suggests the benefits of integrated education, integrated housing, the expansion of education outside of school, and the role of the arts, including music, film and theatre, to bring together young people in shared spaces and experiences.

Segregated education and housing clearly has negative consequences on society. "We still have a society that is as segregated as it ever was," says Peter Osborne. "We still have new people coming through, young people reaching maturity, becoming adults, that are living in segregated housing, that go to segregated education.

"Our system has the greatest degree of social engineering there's ever been."

"Because of those things, they are socialised in a way that is segregated. Our system has the greatest degree of social engineering that there's ever been. I am a strong advocate for young people learning and developing together. I'm told - because I would be a supporter of that - I want to socially engineer. It's not me that socially engineers, it's the people who created a system a hundred or more years ago that segregate our children when they're four or five years old. That's the greatest degree of social engineering you could get."

Almost echoing the conclusions of Mark Daly, Peter also complains that the scale of ambition and action in Northern Ireland is simply inadequate. "We have a shared housing policy. But over two terms of an Assembly, 10 years, the policy around shared housing, its aim is to build 487 houses in 10 years in shared housing schemes. In that same 10 years, we will build over 60,000 units. So our shared housing policy has an ambition which equates to less than 1% of total housing. I could make an argument that that is going to reinforce the segregation in housing because they're replacing houses in areas that were less segregated in the 1940s and '50s and '60s than they are today. There's just not enough [shared housing].

"And then in one of those shared housing units two years ago, UVF flags go up and two families are intimidated out. We allow those flags to continue to fly and people move out of shared housing. That area will not be a shared housing area in a year or two unless we really defend the policy that is supposed to be there. We'll abandon it as somewhere that people don't want to live in if, in this case, they're from a Catholic background.

"We need to take dramatic, bold policy decisions that are going to structurally change this society. Managing conflict and managing division is one thing, it's what the Community Relations Council does with the relatively small amount of funding that it gives out, it promotes cross community activity. What we need to do is tackle the causes of segregation and we haven't done that yet."

Peter argues that more must be done to protect social integration and shared housing. He says: "I think the law and legal guidance is very clear. You cannot erect things on lampposts. There are a number of laws that make it clear that they should not be there. I don't think it's about *what* flags are up. It is unlawful to put material like that on a lamppost. I understand how difficult that is. It's not just a policing issue, it's for other agencies, too.

"And can you take those flags down everywhere? That would be a huge challenge because of the number of flags that are up. But when you come to a shared housing area, you need to implement the law. When the law says you cannot put flags up, it is even stronger when it comes to flags that are related to a proscribed illegal organisation, especially to intimidate. Those flags should be coming down in shared housing areas. We should be zero tolerant in that, when the flags go up give it a day or two to see if people would take them down themselves. If they don't, they should come down.

"A couple of years ago, they went up in June. In one street they came down in September. On another street, more of a shared housing area, it took Santa Claus to come in December for people dressed as Santa to go up to put Christmas decorations up and while they were doing that, they took the UVF flags down, six months later. That's just not acceptable and it's certainly not acceptable in one of the flagship shared housing areas. There needs to be courage and decision-making in those areas to say it's just zero tolerance: there will be no symbols like that going up in shared housing areas.

"There's something we need to reflect on, how we encourage more people to want to live in shared housing areas because we need to increase the numbers. I think 487 over 10 years is too little. I keep coming back to financial incentives for people living in those shared housing areas. I'd be open to other ideas, but it's certainly something that's there that may well help to increase the number of people living in those areas. But when they're there, they need to be protected around flags and emblems.

"Think of what it says when for two or three months of the year it's okay to put flags up that identify an area as for one community."

"In Northern Ireland there are very few council areas that are exclusively unionist or nationalist. Most council areas will be very close in make-up. Think of what it says when you say for two or three months of the year, it's okay to put flags up that identify an area as one particular side of the community or other. What you're actually saying is to that minority community, 'Keep your head down for those number of months. Put up with it. Tolerate being intimidated. Don't go into certain areas. Just keep your head down and don't show yourself to be from that minority community.'. That's not acceptable in any society, and it certainly should be the aim to be building a society where we don't accept that."

"Decision-making is naturally sectarian because our politics are naturally sectarian. Decisions become about one community winning, one community losing. That goes to the heart of integration."

Andrew McCracken observes: "When I think about housing, it immediately makes me think about just how we manage where money flows, for social housing, how we decide what doctors' surgeries to have, how we decide what leisure centres to have, the decision-making that is naturally sectarian because our politics is naturally sectarian tends to mitigate all those decisions to be about one community winning and one community losing and that goes to the heart of integration. So yes, housing, but then yes to those systems that we current manage as being about orange and green and how can we get more normal politics, whether that's local council or whatever Stormont-related government we have to try to get to the root of that."

Integrated education – bringing together children of different religions, and of none - is equally important. Alexandra de la Torre explains: "I was a development officer in the Northern Ireland Council for Integrated Education and I see integrated education as the way forward. I don't think integrated education excludes other cultural identities. Integrated education enhances in an amazing way all our differences, enhances and celebrates all communities. Integrated education is one of those spaces where you see that it is happening.

"We cannot have any more of this divided society and integrated education doesn't go against choice, parents' choice, it doesn't go against cultural identity. When you go to an integrated school you see that both communities have things celebrated equally, where children have the opportunity to say what they are and what they want and it is such an amazing space for children to grow and learn together. Perhaps the next challenge for integrated education is to incorporate all of these policies, initiatives, to integrate children from ethnic minorities."

While both integrated education and integrated housing are important, some believe that having dedicated bodies to promote integrated education has given it more impetus and focus than is the case with shared housing. "I would like to see a strategic body focusing especially on housing," says Father Martin Magill.

The existing policy on shared housing is weak not only because the scale is too small, but because both in terms of planning and enforcement, it fails to prevent supposed 'shared housing' areas becoming the focus of conflicting territorial ambitions of paramilitary groups. Building new estates at existing interface areas is perhaps doomed to failure at present, whereas there is an alternative of promoting city centre apartments that create the opportunity for naturally mixed communities.

Martin agrees this may be more productive. "Yes, maybe we do need to begin with some of the easier ones where we encourage that without it becoming social engineering," he says.

Martin favours the formation of a strategic body promoting shared housing, which involves the Housing Executive and individual housing associations. He continues: "I would like to see something more strategic, what I call 'community champions'. I am aware of people who have purposely chosen to live in areas that wouldn't be necessarily their first choice.... That whole sense of purposely choosing to live in this area to make a difference. We need more of that."

Some practitioners believe that storytelling and the arts can help improve our understanding of our history, while improving empathy across the divided community. Maureen Hetherington says: "I was the founder of Towards Understanding and Healing[19] and that's dealing with the past through storytelling and positive and counter dialogue. I see that's core to moving society forward, re-humanising those we have demonised and hearing the human cost on what has happened here.

"I do think it's one of the most powerful ways in which young people and adults can start to think differently about the past. If you live in a ghetto, in a segregated society, you have a perception of who the enemy are. If you don't move outside that you don't hear the narratives outside of your own narrative, of your own community. You build a picture and everybody else is

---

19 Towards Understanding and Healing is a project of The Junction.

the perceived enemy and you're the victim. To expose yourself to the different narratives gives you the opportunity to change the story you tell yourself in that re-humanising and integrating that different story. You can start to change what you've heard from your peers, your family, your community and it can help you to start to move on and think differently. That is about creating the critical thinking skills in which you say well, that can't all be true, or you start to investigate."

Maureen believes it is important that people think for themselves, rather than just receive ideas. "It's getting enough people to engage actively and start to ask critical questions. Asking critical questions of our politicians. Our deeply segregated society, the way that our politicians behave to each other and with each other, it's hugely contentious and creates a lot of ill feeling. It's done deliberately in coming up to voting times - that level of hostility goes up. I have to accept there isn't a level of maturity in the political world here - it takes a generation or two generations before you can develop a mature political system."

Healing through forgiveness and understanding are possible, suggests Father Martin Magill. He gives as an example the events where Jo Berry - daughter of Anthony Berry MP, who was killed in the Brighton Grand Hotel bomb – shares a panel with Patrick Magee, the Brighton bomber. "The focus was on the two of them, but what happened afterwards acted as a catalyst for people to come and tell their stories," recalls Martin about one of the meetings they attended. "They wanted to tell their stories. That whole sense, first of all of being able to be heard, that the value of other people hearing that story and trying to understand why people got involved in the first place is really important."

Claire Sugden makes a related point. "It is important to know where people come from. Sociologically, we are all products of our environments and our upbringings. I don't think anyone is born bad, it's the journey and the path that they have gone through their lives. It is really important that we do look back. It's not even with the purpose of justifying some of the actions, or some of the things that happened in Northern Ireland, but it does get us to a place where we're de-sensitising our past a bit. To move forward is key, because the [three years of Assembly suspension] inflamed anger." People with past experience of the Troubles were angry at the thought that their children and grandchildren were not being governed in ways that secure a better future.

When reflecting on the past, it is also essential not to focus just on those who were in the front line of the conflict, but also to consider women and families. Alexandra de la Torre observes: "I did my PhD on the role of civil societies in peace building and I looked at the role of women during the conflict. Until very recently, women didn't feel - or this is what I captured in my interviews - that they were victims of the conflict because they weren't necessarily engaged in violence, or that they had to suffer the consequence of family loss. Fathers were imprisoned. And all these day-by-day situations that they [women] had to deal with, but so many here said, 'Well, this is what I had to do' and that's it.

"But that is part of the discourse of being a victim, when your everyday life changed because of the conflict. And some women's organisations are doing amazing work trying to bring these stories back into oral history projects, to recognise and let society know that those women were also victims of the conflict. Whatever you do in terms of transitional justice, to try to accommodate systems within the political system to accommodate the needs of the victims and also to move on, you need to provide those spaces for women to be recognised as victims of the conflict."

Both Simon Hamilton and Máirtín Ó Muilleoir are concerned that there was little contact of any kind between MLAs of different parties during times when the Assembly was not sitting. This made the building of partnerships and compromises even more difficult. Speaking during a long period of suspension, Máirtín observes: "Having no Assembly is a real hindrance in terms of building relations among political leaders because you don't see people in the corridors or in the cafes or whatever, you don't get to know them, you don't hear them speak or anything else".

He adds: "I think there's less dialogue and interaction and if you're asking me how to solve that, I don't know. I'm sure people would come up with a hundred ways. Somebody said, 'Oh, I'll just pick up the phone'. But there's less dialogue. The term I've used is 'all bridges are down'. If you ask me now to ring a DUP MLA, first of all I don't know half of them because they were elected after the Assembly election, I've never met them. I see their pictures in the paper occasionally and I'm amazed, I'm saying, 'My God, who is this?'. But if you ask me now frankly could I ring a DUP MLA and ask them to co-sponsor an activity for Inspire Mental Health or PIPS, suicide prevention, I don't have a DUP MLA I could talk to."

Simon Hamilton agrees, saying that in the absence of an Assembly "there's not even a place where politicians from across the country can sit and have any sort of a debate". Even more significantly, Simon admits that the Executive did far too little in binding society together. He observes: "This sounds maybe a bit ridiculous saying it out loud – but I have thought for a while now that it's odd that a power sharing executive of Sinn Féin and the DUP, with all the difficulties that were there and the effort that had been

---

"It's odd that a power-sharing executive of Sinn Féin and the DUP didn't prioritise peace-building and developing a shared society. We maybe thought that just doing power sharing was enough, without realising that you had to go much, much further than that."

---

put into coming together, the symbolism that was inherent within that in itself, didn't actually prioritise peace building and trying to develop a shared society. Even trying to work out what we meant by 'a shared society' or 'a more integrated society'. It didn't feel that that was always our priority.

"Maybe what I'm trying to say is that we maybe thought that just doing it, ie power sharing, was enough in itself without realising that you had to go much, much further beyond that. You have to be careful of course, we can't go further than our community any more than Sinn Féin can go further than theirs, but there was and there remains in spite of it all, a yearning. People don't talk about it as shared society or more integrated – just normality. That is what they call it. There'll be a difference in people's definition of 'normality', but they do want it. Most people don't want the continuation of what happened before. They don't want to go back to what happened before. They want it to be better. They don't want their kids to grow up and their grandkids to grow up in a society which is as divided as the one that they had."

Máirtín believes that given the significance of religion in Northern Ireland, church service attendance can be symbolically important. He explains: "I'm not a person of faith, but I have high regard for the Protestant churches in particular and the work they do with wounded and vulnerable people and those on the margins. But there's another little thing, when you go into a church the people feel obliged to welcome you. So I've been to church with the Reverend Mervyn Gibson, who is a chaplain of the Orange Order and a former Special Branch man and Mervyn would always welcome me very warmly to service and that's an interesting discovery to me, that instead of trying to meet people away from the church, if you want to try and find a way to break the ice or to seek the security of an encounter where you can maybe make some progress rather than it being a shouting match, actually going to church with people is in my view a good way to do it. It has to be done sincerely and with authenticity and genuine, but I have found that going to church is one way that you can try to learn a bit more about people and try to understand their perspective and at the same time you know you won't be chased."

Naomi Long makes a more secular point about how social integration can be achieved from a variety of different policy measures. "We know, for example, that public transport is crucial," she says. "That people feeling safe, feeling that it's efficient and effective, but also knowing where it starts and stops. So, for example, more people now will travel east to west in the city because of the Glider system, because they know that they can get on the bus on the Falls Road, come to the Upper Newtownards Road, or to Stormont, or wherever it might be - it's one bus journey, there's no changes, there's no getting lost, they know where they're going to get off and then they can get back on the bus and go straight back and there's a sense of security and safety in that, but it's also simple and straightforward. And so what we have seen is people exploring areas outside their natural comfort zones. So to be able to do that, you've got to facilitate that movement of people around the city and that's important."

Derry's Peace Bridge had a similar impact in helping to bring together a divided city, by connecting what had been perceived to be separate communities.

Another key message is that we must not be too impatient for progress. Simon observes: "We probably haven't taken collectively the time to sit back and say this is a 50-year job probably here. Nobody wants to hear that it's a 50-year job, but that's maybe at the low end of the scale."

"We are in a process that will last at least 50 years."

Peter Osborne makes a similar estimation, with an added warning: "We need to be real about what this peace process is about," he says. "First of all, we are in a process that will last at least 50 years. Some people think when the Agreement was signed we had peace. We don't. Some people think it would take 10 or 20 years. It won't. It will take generations and it will be at least 50 years. So 20 years on from the Good Friday Agreement, we are less than halfway through this process. I say that because we need to have the context right, there are no quick fixes, but we also need to understand that it can go backwards as well as forwards. There is no inevitable forward flow to the peace in Northern Ireland and we are in a very serious situation."

Speaking at a time of Assembly suspension, Peter warned darkly: "At the minute, at best, we are standing still."

CHAPTER FIVE
RECOGNISING DEMOGRAPHIC CHANGE

"We are all minorities in Northern Ireland now."
Peter Osborne.

Northern Ireland appears to be in a state of flux, with Brexit in particular raising questions in the minds of the population about their personal identity, while also reinforcing and antagonising divisions as communities unhappy with the result or the process blame each other.

Symptoms of that flux can be shown in the annual Life and Times Survey – and also underline the danger of giving undue reliance on the results of a single population or opinion survey. In the 2018 Northern Ireland Life and Times Survey[20], half of adults surveyed did not primarily identify themselves as either unionist or nationalist. Yet the following year's survey indicated significantly different results. This found more respondents designated as unionists than nationalists (33% compared to 22%), but with a larger group (39%) saying they were neither. More respondents (44%) regarded themselves as Protestants than called themselves Catholics (34%), with a significant group (22%) being neither.

There are other signs of a changing political and religious demography. Only one of the four Belfast MPs is now a unionist: three identify as nationalist in a city for long seen as a bastion of unionism. On Belfast City Council, too, unionists are now in a minority: with those who identify as neither unionist nor nationalist having almost as many councillors as those who identify as unionist. (In the 2019 local government elections, 24 Belfast seats were won by people who identify as nationalists; 19 by unionists; and 17 by councillors who do not identify as either.)

Those trends are set to continue and accelerate. There is now near equality in the working age population between those who identify as Protestant, and those who identified as Catholic. In 2017 (the most recent published survey), some 42% of the working age population identified as Protestant, while 41% identified as Catholic and 17% did not identify as either.[21] (It should be noted that there remains a wider difference when it comes to the employment rate, which was 70% for Protestants and 67% for Catholics.) Amongst school children, there is a majority who are Catholic – 51% are

---

20 https://www.ark.ac.uk/nilt/2018/
21 https://www.executiveoffice-ni.gov.uk/sites/default/files/publications/execoffice/lfs-religion-report-2017.pdf

Catholic, compared to just 37% who are Protestant.[22]

Peter Osborne observes that "we are all minorities in Northern Ireland now". He continues: "There is no majority. We're all minorities. The only way you make this place work from a unionist perspective is to help reconcile the people in Northern Ireland so they can work together better. If you're from a nationalist or republican background, exactly the same argument applies before you can get into any substantial conversation about changing the constitutional status, or uniting the island as a whole in one political framework."

Mike Nesbitt agrees. "What concerns me from a unionist perspective is that we are in danger of becoming the famous frog that Charles Handy used to talk about. He was a business guru who said if you take a frog and put it in a pan of cold water and very, *very* slowly heat it to boiling point, the frog dies because at no point does it realise the environment around it has changed until the point it's too late. Unionism needs to look and recognise that the environment around us is changing.

"The demographics are changing. That does not mean a united Ireland is inevitable, but it is something we need to be aware of. Scottish nationalism is a threat to the union, English nationalism is a threat to the union and I would go as far as to say that I believe the DUP and some of their policies, attitudes and tone is a long term threat to the union. So I would like to see civic unionism becoming more active.

Mike adds: "We have to recognise first of all that nobody is going away. We could all get cryogenically frozen, five years, 15, 50 years, but when we come back there are still going to be Irish republicans and nationalists, there are going to be British unionists and loyalists and people who describe themselves as 'other' on this little postage stamp on planet earth. So we need to learn to share. We need to recognise nobody owns this piece of planet earth. If you go back to the first page of the Belfast Agreement where it talks about building new relationships, the first value was tolerance of each other. It's time to move beyond tolerance because to me tolerance is simply saying 'I will accept you're here. I won't necessarily be positive about it, I just won't be negative about it'. We need to learn to be positive and use our diversity as a strength. And there has to be political leadership for that."

> "It's time to move beyond tolerance."

Mike warns that unionism has to be more outward facing. He says: "I would strongly encourage unionism to engage because it is my experience, not only as a politician but before that as a journalist, that unionism is not good at engaging with others. The best example is 25 years ago, Gerry Adams

22 https://www.bbc.co.uk/news/uk-northern-ireland-43823506

got his 48-hour visa from Bill Clinton to go to a conference in New York, a conference that Jim Molyneux of the Ulster Unionists and Ian Paisley of the DUP had already signed up to speak at. But when Gerry Adams got his ticket the two unionist leaders not only withdrew from the conference, they cancelled their flights and stayed home, leaving the pitch clear to Gerry Adams. And then unionists complain the White House is green.

"What do you expect when you only hear one side of the story? Paisley and Molyneux should have gone to New York. They should have had their own event before the conference and said, 'When you go across the road, ask Mr Adams about Jean McConville and the Disappeared. Ask him about Bloody Friday. Ask him about La Mon, a napalm bomb on civilians in a hotel.'. Americans would have understood. So, I am for engaging, and not just to rant, as I may have just ranted against the former president of Sinn Féin, but to engage and say, 'We are confident about who we are and what we stand for, let's talk, let's see where there's commonality'. And there might be a lot more than we imagine."

Then there is the challenge of how our society deals with the continued existence – and strength – of paramilitaries. The Good Friday Agreement deferred that challenge for another day, but that day has yet to come. Observers have argued that the former Social Investment Fund (SIF) indirectly financed some paramilitaries. There is also clear evidence that on occasions active paramilitary groups have been able to exert influence on political parties. It was widely suggested that it was the opposition of loyalist paramilitary groups that vetoed an Irish Language Act in 2018, that was broadly agreed by the main parties and would have enabled the Assembly to reconvene. And the Ulster Unionist Party indicated that threats from loyalist paramilitaries led to it not running a candidate in the North Belfast constituency in the 2019 General Election. (Republican paramilitaries also exercise a negative influence in politics on both sides of the border, including through involvement in major crime gangs. The Real IRA has engaged in the Dublin drug trade and a former member of the Continuity IRA was alleged to be involved in the Kinahan-Hutch gang warfare.)

Senator Mark Daly observes that "some of the community leaders in both communities are community leaders by day and then they're involved in criminality by night". He continues: "Most people are doing great work

> "Some of the community leaders in both communities are community leaders by day and then they're involved in criminality by night."

but there are some who are not and they are giving a romanticised view... of the Troubles and in some communities, the loyalist community, you're a paramilitary leader during the Troubles you had standing in your community, you were protecting your community, you were in the UDR, you were in the British Army, or you were in the RUC. You had standing. You had a well-paid job and there was that idea in the loyalist community that in some ways they were undefeated and therefore they will never be defeated and that view was being put out there. And then on the republican side, this is unfinished business, and again, young people who have no memory of the harm of the Troubles will be exploited by people, adults, who want to achieve their own ends and give this glorified view of the past."

But perhaps the biggest challenge facing the political structures of Northern Ireland is the limited commitment to making them work, or achieving a rapprochement across the communities.

Ken Good, the former Church of Ireland Bishop of Derry and Raphoe, has made the point that for an avowedly Christian society, it is surprising how little forgiveness there is in Northern Ireland. He concedes: "It's very difficult for me to talk about this because I've never lost a family member to violence. I grew up in Cork and I'm an outsider to that extent. So I have to tread softly and carefully here, because for people who have at first hand confronted the death of a loved one through violence, it's holy ground and I don't want to be preaching at them or above them in any judgemental kind of way and make their suffering worse. But I've also travelled to Africa and seen in Uganda, in particular, where there was huge tribal conflict and mass murder, how there seems to be a capacity to forgive in a way that there isn't as much here. Now there is forgiveness here too, but not as much as I've seen elsewhere.

"One of my Archdeacons, Robert Miller, has written with Father Paul Farren a book called *Forgiveness Remembers*[23] and they're saying that forgiveness isn't about forgetting. You don't forget and you shouldn't have to forget. You remember, but somehow forgiveness is liberating. Unforgiveness is the opposite. It can be ensnaring and it can hold the person who is not able to forgive. It can hold them down more than it holds the person down who they are feeling a grudge against. These are big spiritual themes and I'm not preaching at anybody when I say this, but I think it is something that as Christian churches we have to confront more robustly."

> "Forgiveness isn't about forgetting."

---

23 Forgiveness Remembers by Paul Farren and Robert Miller

CHAPTER SIX
MENTAL HEALTH

"Now people are getting time and space to think: an awful lot of the trauma is coming back out again." Aideen McGinley.

While the perception of Northern Ireland is of divided communities, one aspect of society is common across many different backgrounds: a mental health crisis. More people died from suicide in Northern Ireland since the Good Friday Agreement, than from violence during the entire length of the Troubles.[24]

"Northern Ireland spends just 5% of its total health budget on mental health, which is less than half of the proportion allocated in England, despite estimates of local mental health problems being 25% higher than in England," explained the Pivotal think-tank.[25]

It would be wrong to suggest a simple explanation for the reasons for such a high incidence of poor mental health. Factors include lack of access to early intervention, excessive use of medication, cultural acceptance of alcohol addiction, inter-generational trauma and the direct and indirect impact of events during the Troubles.

"The way I see it is that often people can be united in pain, trauma, emotional pain," observes Senator Frances Black. "We all know, particularly within the six counties, people have been impacted by the conflict. The trauma that comes out of that can be carried down the generations. When I was in college, I did a piece of work on it and when I started to look at it, particularly during the conflict, I talked to a few community organisations. I was very interested in the field of addiction and how that manifested itself.

"I realised during the conflict there was a lot of prescription medication given out to people and you can understand why. I know myself, even travelling to the north you could feel the tension. You could feel at any point there could be something that's going to go off, or there could be an explosion, or you see the Army going around with guns. Even though people get used to it, it can be scary, particularly if you're a young child.

"If you have a partner that went to jail, or any family member, or a family member killed or shot, there's huge trauma. It was dealt with by giving out prescription medication, huge amounts of medication given out. That can

24 https://www.theguardian.com/uk-news/2018/feb/20/northern-ireland-suicides-troubles-death-toll
25 https://www.pivotalppf.org/cmsfiles/Publications/Moving-forward-report--web-version.pdf

impact the next generation. If you have maybe the father goes to jail and the mother goes on prescription [drugs], she's got five kids or six kids, she's trying to struggle, she trying to get through life, the trauma of what's going on around her, she sees it everywhere, whatever community you're from the impact is the same.

"You start taking prescription medication and the children nearly lose both parents because the parent who's on the prescription medication cannot be present. They can go through the motions and maybe cook the dinner, but [they are] not really present.

"Often the eldest child will look after the rest of the kids and there's this ongoing legacy that's carried on down. That's what trauma does and what addiction does. That's what unhealthy relationships with prescription drugs can do.

"When I went into the different communities and I met with different communities I met with people from both sides, the issues are the same, the heartache is the same, the mental health in particular. When the [Oireachtas] Good Friday Implementation Committee went up to visit, we went into west Belfast and we talked to the community there... then we went into the Shankill Road and the issues were quite the same. When I started to talk to them about mental health and the impact on young people, about what was going on, the deprivation, the lack of housing, the lack of jobs and all of those things, they started to come alive. Within that meeting, people started to talk about mental health.

"I remember one man saying he was with a group of young men and asked them, 'What kind of a job would you love to do?' and they said 'My dream job is to drive a van for a local supermarket'. My heart went out. And they talked a lot about mental health. One man talked about driving down a certain road where at one time a bomb went off and he still goes into the trauma of what that felt like and he still goes into that hyper-vigilance. As a result he had to go to his doctor to get medication. It's just a vicious cycle that can be carried down to the next generation.

"I genuinely believe that if those issues, if we started off from that level in working with the communities and bringing people together, talking about their anxieties, their stresses, their worries. I remember in north Belfast one time going to a huge event around suicide and people from both communities who'd lost family members - the pain and heartache were the same. People got up and spoke about their loved one and it didn't matter what community they came from. They could identify with each other through that pain.

"The Rise Foundation[26] is the charitable organisation I set up in 2009. We went up to Rathlin Island[27], we ran programmes. We ran cross-border, cross-community programmes. What that meant was you would have ten people in a room cross-community, but we also brought people up from Dublin or Donegal or wherever. The Rise Foundation supports family members who have somebody they love with an addiction problem, with an alcohol, drug or gambling problem. Anybody that has a family member in addiction is heartbroken.

"What I discovered through that programme was that people could identify with each other, identified with the heartache, with the sadness, with the loss they had, but they would bring in their own heartache to being part of the conflict. That has to come out. What happened to them and their family. You would have unionists, nationalists who would talk and people from down south would have had no idea what happened in the north during the conflict. It was amazing the support they gave each other and almost held each other - it was powerful to watch. I have no answers with regard to how you do that on a larger scale. But it's certainly worth a conversation."

Frances adds: "We know the suicide rates are huge in certain areas in the north, but we also know the suicide rates in Cork are huge. Suicide is something that nobody understands unless you go through it yourself. If you have somebody that you know or love, the ripple effect is devastating, not only to the family, but also to the whole community. There's huge levels of suicide across the island of Ireland. Then you have mental health, people who suffer with anxiety, depression, so many different mental health issues. When we say the words 'mental health' we have this image of somebody who's after having a nervous breakdown. That's not what I'm talking about. I would have had depression many, many years ago and I struggled through it and I would consider that a mental health issue. You don't know what's wrong with you, but when you bring people together on that level it can bond people and barriers go down."

Senator Mark Daly observes: "Senator Frances Black did an excellent piece where she talked about the intergenerational trauma where in fact there are now more people being traumatised by the Troubles and people who weren't even born during the Troubles are being traumatised by the consequences of the Troubles because their parents who had gone through the Troubles who might have lost a loved one, some of them could be suffering from mental health problems as a result, Post-Traumatic Stress Disorder, alcohol and drug

---

26 The Rise Foundation
27 Rathlin Island is off the north coast of County Antrim. Frances Black's father originates from there.

addiction, and that then is having effect on the next generation. So now we are having a pyramid effect where there are more and more people being affected by the Troubles in a generation that wasn't even born at the time.

"The return on investment in mental health services is very important, but that requires structure. There are a lot of good people who set up something either on the Shankill Road or the Falls Road but then there's nothing over in east Belfast or there's nothing in Newry or there's nothing in Ballymena for people who suffer the same trauma. So it doesn't have the roll-out in the way that it should and that's why you need a plan. Because, of course, policy neglect seldom goes unpunished."

There is an explanation as to why the trauma of the Troubles can have a delayed impact. Professor Siobhan O'Neill told the New York Times: "For

"During the Troubles, the suicide rates in Northern Ireland were actually lower than they are now."

anxiety disorders and PTSD, 22 years was the average time between symptom onset and treatment, because people didn't want to talk and ruminate over the terrible things they went through. During the Troubles, the suicide rates in Northern Ireland were actually lower than they are now.

"It seems that the conflict gave those who may have otherwise been suicidal, a sense of purpose — to fight, to live. But when the Troubles ended, many people struggled to make sense of what all that fighting was about and what had been achieved, and then the suicide rates went up."[28] She added that of 28 countries and regions participating in the 2017 World Mental Health Survey, Northern Ireland had the highest rate of PTSD.

MLA Claire Sugden believes that Northern Ireland fails to recognise the scale of the trauma legacy we are continuing to face. She says: "One thing that really struck me in my work as minister of justice when I was meeting a lot of victims and their families, was that the trauma from what had happened - and trauma is such a big part of conflict and it's appalling that as a post-conflict society we have never even considered how we dealt with our trauma and still aren't 20 years later - but that trauma seems to get passed from generation to generation. If we are genuinely going to reconcile we have to break that trauma at some point. "

Mental health is a policy area which might be argued has been neglected, or at least not addressed sufficiently. Aideen McGinley observes: "Mental

28 https://www.nytimes.com/2019/12/01/world/europe/northern-ireland-suicide.html

health in Northern Ireland is abominable. I'm involved in a mental health charity and it is shocking the levels of suicide, particularly of young men. The waiting lists, the reliance on voluntary activity. I was at a conference recently in Whitehall around Embedding Wellbeing and they were using the example about Northern Ireland being the happiest place in the UK. And I said, 'Yes and it has the highest number of people on anti-depressants'."

Aideen is concerned that the scale of the problem is not being recognised. "We're facing a crisis at the minute," she says. "One of the reasons we're in the chasm we're in is that a lot of people of my era who would have been involved in the early Troubles and right through it and worked through it now are coming to retirement age where all of a sudden people kept busy, people lived their lives. They created the opportunities for their kids and their grandkids and they got on with life and they were on a treadmill and it kept them going. Now people are getting time and space to think: an awful lot of the trauma is coming back out again. I was talking to somebody recently who said there's a 22-year gap. It's been 22 years and all of a sudden people are coming and saying 'I have a problem'. Some of it's about we haven't let ourselves remember. We are coming to a point where some of the political chaos is making us remember and retrace back to our [past] and working through it."

In some instances, Julieann Campbell observes, people who had severely damaging experiences during the Troubles may decide to closet the recollections away: "there's so many people out there that are afraid to maybe speak because it might re-traumatise them," she says. Julieann adds: "The trauma is there either way. If you stay quiet, it's an internal trauma. And if you share it, then it almost feels like you're sharing the burden and that has to help in the long run."

Mark Daly suggests we should not over-worry about re-traumatising people who experienced horrors during the Troubles – he argues that they remain traumatised, so will not be re-traumatised. The important thing, Mark argues, is that we provide sufficient services for people in need. He says: "Some people may never want to access the services but the thing is the services need to be there and some people don't even know they are traumatised and again, some people would seek justice, some seek to confront someone, some would seek to bury it. And that requires again the Victims Commission and all that and the fact that the system is even holding back information on state security grounds means that people are being traumatised more, they're becoming victims again of the system and literally the campaigns are being passed on from one generation to the next as the generation who lost a loved one, a brother or sister, as they're dying off then you have their sons and daughters, nieces and nephews, who are taking up the campaign to get justice, to get the truth and that again has a huge drain on them as human beings and their futures as well because they are not getting the justice which they deserve and it is having a knock-on effect on society.

"So it really is about making sure that you have programmes in place but not having a belief that one size fits all - you have to tailor the programmes and there is no simple solution but ignoring it is not the solution. And, in some instances, that's what the Irish government and the British government have done in terms of dealing with the legacies of the past, they have not dealt with them in the way that they should. Say for example in the case of some of those people who were killed during the Troubles, they haven't received an inquest. Legally required by the law of the land to have an inquest, but no inquest was carried out. The basics weren't even done."

Julieann Campbell believes that talking about the experiences of the past, as she did, can help people to deal with them. She says: "It has been life changing for a few of them that just had never dealt with what happened to them in the past. And even having one person listening to them - well two in the case of this project because it was me and Carol Cunningham - but that acknowledgement, it was a few hours of our life, but it changed someone else's life. That's not to be sniffed at. That's a significant achievement in their lives, that they were able to speak and be heard and feel that they can start... what's the word... I can't say 'move on' because you can't move on, but start to deal with what was in their head."

She adds: "I would say [it's] a catharsis. It's always a word I use - there was a catharsis involved in it and I would find that with a lot of storytelling work, that people get a lot out of just speaking and recounting their own experiences. It goes back to that, 'Oh, I don't have much to say', and then they start speaking and it's unbelievably, historically important stuff. So while it's traumatising, especially on the *Unheard Voices*, we had trauma support in place and counselling services and things like that, just in case. We didn't want to reopen raw wounds and then leave these people to it. That was part of the deal, if you need help, we will help you."

Jo Egan was the dramatist of the Crack in Everything, in which family members spoke on stage of the impact of the Troubles on their relatives. Jo reflects: "Counselling and psychotherapy and the *correct* type of treatment for post-traumatic stress is very, very important. I don't personally believe that we have enough counsellors who can do that and if you speak to somebody like Siobhan O'Neill she backs that up and I'm lucky that I have a couple of close friends who have gone through many years of training to be trauma therapists. So I'm aware of just how much work they've had to do.

"But we can bring in as many people – and that's a very important part of this - we can bring as many people into the counselling room as we like, people want to be *heard* and they want to be heard in society. They want their stories recognised and we need to recognise and hear the stories. I know people will become exhausted by it and I think we have to become more and more skilled and adept. I think if we keep repeating that style of theatre, it's not going to work because there's got be something for an audience to be able to catch on – we don't want to do 'Troubles porn'. You don't want that because that's what people have done in the past.

> "People want to be heard and they want to be heard in society."

"But you need to fall back then on the dramatic skills. If you don't have people who know how to dramatise something properly, then you'll either have people turning away and not listening or you'll have people exhausted. And what happens then is that people will go back into thinking that their story is not valid."

The absence of counselling services and trauma support in the past presents its own continuing difficulties. Freya McClements – co-author of *Children of the Troubles* – explains: "Families over and over would say things, 'There was nothing. There was no counselling back then'. How did family members cope? It was through alcohol. Just anecdotally, the prevalence of mental health issues within families is really significant. That distance is a really key thing, because families would always make the distinction between that there was nothing back then, but there are families now who maybe lost a child 30 or 40 years ago who are only now feeling that they are at the point where they can go and do something about it, or go out and talk about it. That's really significant and that idea of it being more reflective is definitely true because, even to do a book like this and to do a project like this. It would have been difficult to do even 10 years ago.

"The last child - and we take child as being 16 and under - by our criteria who was killed was Michael McIlveen in 2006. So there's a 13 year span [to when the interview was conducted]. It's about giving space to reflect and talk about things that really haven't been talked about. And that's a key thing as well. This kind of thing wasn't talked about and there are families who would say things like, 'Until it came to our door, we didn't really know anything about the Troubles'. You were aware it was going on but we didn't pay attention to it because you were just concentrating on living, you were concentrating on raising your family, you were concentrating on keeping them out of trouble and then suddenly there's a bomb, or something happens and suddenly it comes to their door in a sense.

"So there was the element of that keeping going and now because we are in more peaceful times there's that space and there's that ability to reflect and there's also, in some cases, there's the importance of acknowledgement and that was one of the big things about the book compared to what I do day-to-day as a journalist. There were families who would say, 'Look, we have never spoken to anybody before but because this is a book we want this down in the book because it is going to be a record of the children and we want people to know.'. There are mothers and fathers, siblings out there who are really elderly now, in 10 years' time they are not going to be here. So, there's a merit in getting that down in print now."

Sophie Long suggests that the experience of this type of storytelling illustrates the potential value of an oral archive of the Troubles. "A lot of the Stormont House Agreement[29] was really good. The idea of an Oral History Archive is brilliant. People involved in local projects say, 'Oh, I haven't told my story before and it's been 30 years.'. To me that's insane. Imagine carrying that round with you. There was a couple of things the families weren't happy with about the cut-off date for the start of investigations, but if you're looking for solutions, both the victims' sector and the academics working in that field, they have put forward proposals saying, 'Look victims are a diverse group, they want different things, but here are the range of things which they need in order to feel some sort of peace'. And those are the things that we need to do."

> "Victims are a diverse group, they want different things."

While it can be positive to consider past events, we also need to consider the impact of stories on future generations. Maureen Hetherington of the Junction warns: "A child has to learn empathy and if a child isn't taught it at a very young age, it grows up without that knowledge of how it has to develop empathy. That'll extend to areas of racism, sectarianism, prejudice and discrimination. It's one of the areas where parents have to take responsibility about what they pass on to their children. The inter-generational passing on is very important to be challenged as well and we're doing work in that

---

29 https://www.gov.uk/government/publications/the-stormont-house-agreement

area where we're trying to do education and training programmes raising awareness of what the parents pass on to their children. If we're trying to create a new generation of young people coming up that don't hold onto prejudices, we're in trouble. We carry the conflict on.

"It's heartbreaking to me sometimes when I hear someone say, 'Well, if I don't get justice I have so many children, I have so many grandchildren, and they'll take up the challenge to find justice' and I'm thinking, 'What are we doing to our children? What are we doing to our grandchildren? When are we going to break these cycles of violence, prejudice and discrimination?'. I

"There's stuff we have to let go of."

don't believe we have to draw a line in the sand, but we have to get people to think differently about how we start working towards the common good, or the greater good, and compromise and realise there's stuff – this is very difficult to say – there's stuff we have to let go of. We have to learn to let go of things that might be very, very painful if we have any hope for the future of our children. If we care at all about our children and grandchildren, we have to change."

CHAPTER SEVEN
BUILDING ASPIRATION ACROSS SOCIETY

"The role model in some communities is the local
UDA brigadier." Alan Mcbride.

"We have to encourage young people and give them proper role models to aspire to," argues victims' campaigner Alan Mcbride. "Within loyalist communities there's a real shortage of them, because the role model in some communities is the local UDA brigadier or whatever and they are really bad role models. There needs to be somebody within those communities that can stand up and people could follow and they could inspire. But if that doesn't happen, we're looking at generation after generation of educational failure, of unemployment, of poverty, of sectarianism, of all the things that blight those inner city working class loyalist communities."

One of the important points to note about various research projects is that they conclude that working class boys are underachieving at school – and that is true amongst the Protestant and Catholic populations. That, in turn, feeds into the potential for recruitment by dissident paramilitary groups (both loyalist and republican), which can exploit the lack of hope and aspiration amongst male youths without good examination passes, or skills valued in the labour market.

One cause of the crisis is a divided education system – which is split in two ways. Firstly, there is a separation between the schools that mostly serve Catholics and those that are mostly used by Protestant families. Secondly, the system of selection provides an additional division. Research has found that the main factor within selection is class or affluence. Children on free school meals comprise 40.6% of pupils at non-selective schools, compared to 14.3% of grammar school places.[30] (See next chapter.)

Andrew McCracken is concerned about the separation of children by class – through the selective entrance test for grammar schools – even more than he is about separation by religious tradition. He makes the point that family income levels are a strong indicator of whether a child will go to a grammar or non-selective school. Grammar school entrance, in turn, increases the prospect of good GCSE and A level results, university entrance, a professional career and higher income.

---

30 https://www.irishnews.com/news/educationnews/2018/03/28/news/grammar-schools-do-no-better-in-terms-of-pupil-achievement-study-suggests-1288927/

"The education system is a massive issue we need to solve," he says. "The informal transfer test system sorts kids based on whether they're rich or poor and puts the richer kids in one set of schools and the poorer kids in another set of schools. With all respect for the people working really hard on the Protestant/Catholic issue, if you give me a thousand pounds to do something about those problems, I put it onto the class issue, the rich and poor issue, because it gets even less time in the spotlight. But they're one of the biggest predictors.

"Choose a kid at random and say, I want to work out whether that kid's going to a grammar school or not. If they're on free school meals that's the biggest obvious thing that you can point at to say where they're going to go. And that is not right. I don't believe that if you happen to be on free school meals or not it makes you more or less intelligent. I grew up in brilliant, lovely, middle class Bangor and went to grammar school and went to a lovely university in England. I'm now faced with decisions about where I send my own kids, and the overlay of the individual complexity of navigating this terrible system with your own kids and the strategic perspective of this system is just wrong - and I'm endorsing it by even participating in it. I find it completely overwhelming that I don't know the answer to that, but that integration in education, integration of all sorts and education seem to me to be key."

Alan McBride is on the same page. "Again that goes back to the educational underachievement amongst working class males," he says. "I would be an example of that. I left school when I was 16 with no qualifications, well I did CSEs at the time but they were considered to be worth less than an O Level. We, not just Protestants but Catholic kids as well, were let down by the education system. I've heard people championing our education system as the best in Europe and the best in the world. Maybe for some people that's true, but for a lot of people, certainly people in communities that I would have lived in, that's not at all the case."

There is a common assertion, as Alan McBride says, of Northern Ireland having an excellent education system. But the reality is a mixed picture. Northern Ireland's grammar schools provide a base for excellent examination performance by pupils, leading to Northern Ireland having the UK's highest rate of school leavers going to university (in 2017, 33% left NI to study at university in GB[31]). Yet Northern Ireland also has a very high rate of school leavers without the basic skills in English, maths and IT. In other words, the

31 https://www.tcd.ie/Economics/TEP/2019/tep0619.pdf, p27

system is as divided at exit as it is on entry – and again on class lines.

"Large differences in education outcomes are observed when considering the socio-economic status of the families of school leavers," reported the 2019 Northern Ireland Skills Barometer[32]. "Children who are entitled to Free School Meals (FSM) achieve a significantly lower level of academic achievement relative to their peers who are not entitled to FSM. Only 22.6% of non-FSM pupils fail to achieve at least 5 GCSE's grade A*-C including English and maths, compared to 52.5% of FSM pupils."[33]

This point was addressed by recent research. John FitzGerald and Edgard Morgenroth[34] explained Northern Ireland's weak economic situation, its poor levels of output and high levels of fiscal subvention from the British government. They observed: "The key factor behind the poor productivity performance in Northern Ireland has been the low investment in physical and human capital. The failure to reform the education system to reduce the number of early school leavers and increase the numbers of graduates is the single most important factor in the low growth."

Without either graduate degrees or basic skills – and preferably high quality vocational skills – working class boys are left with limited career options. (The issue is mostly about boys, with working class girls significantly outperforming working class boys in the non-selective sector.[35]) Education minister Peter Weir has recently established an advisory group to suggest steps to correct the under-performance. (Another factor may be the challenges facing single parents, for example with almost half [44.3%] of recent births in the Derry City and Strabane District Council areas being to lone parent households.[36])

"Peter Shirlow did a really good piece of research[37] looking at interface areas and I know this about the interface area that I come from myself," comments Linda Ervine. "He said the major problem in these areas was not sectarianism. It was poverty, it was addiction, it was poor health, it was a

---

32 https://www.economy-ni.gov.uk/sites/default/files/publications/economy/Skills-Barometer-2019-Summary-Report.pdf

33 At 40 post-primary schools in Northern Ireland, less than 50% of school leavers in the 2018/19 year achieved 5 GCSEs, including English and Maths, at grades A* to C, which is regarded as a key measure of pupils' success. http://aims.niassembly.gov.uk/questions/printquestionsummary.aspx?docid=303520

34 https://www.tcd.ie/Economics/TEP/2019/tep0619.pdf

35 https://www.ulster.ac.uk/__data/assets/pdf_file/0020/223409/2000_The_Effects_Of_The_Selective_System_Of_Secondary_Education_In_Northern_Ireland_Main_Report.pdf

36 https://www.economy-ni.gov.uk/sites/default/files/publications/economy/Sub-Regional-Skills-Barometer-2019-North.PDF

37 A detailed social analysis of interface areas was conducted by E. Mark Cummings, Peter Shirlow, Brendan Browne, Clare Dwyer, Christine E. Merrilees and Laura K. Taylor.

lack of education, it was lack of opportunity. And unfortunately the area I come from became a dumping ground as well. So you would have a lot of people with a lot of problems and that's not going to be helpful. Interface areas need massive help."

Many other interviewees made similar points – essentially arguing that deprivation must be addressed to counteract the lure of paramilitary leaders as figures to aspire to, providing status and wealth.

Conal McFeely – chief executive of Creggan Enterprises – argues that the current structure of social inequality is replicating the state of society that led to the civil rights demands of the 1960s, which was the prelude to the Troubles. Conal explains: "If we had a proactive civic society, if we had an effective Bill of Rights, if we had policies that addressed economic disadvantage, social disadvantage, educational disadvantage and ensured that was applying right across all those communities, then civic society would be strengthened. We would have a more cohesive society and we could have built and strengthened our peace."

He believes there should be greater support for the type of social enterprise in poorer communities that he has led at the Rath Mor Centre in Derry, creating new opportunities for people without work in deprived areas. Conal explains: "We need to have policies that address where people are - and lots of people in this society are denied the opportunity to go into the world of work. A lot of people are being denied further education opportunities. The economic agenda rolled-out over the last 20 odd years is quite narrow. It is predicated on one economic model. It needs to be much broader. It needs to embrace the social economy as part of creating a mixed and balanced economy.

"It tends to be in working class Protestant and working class Catholic areas where the conflict was fought out. That's where the highest levels of poverty exist and the highest levels of economic inactivity. Our political elite has been following an economic agenda that is not addressing that."

"People have been looking after the few, instead of looking after the many. The private sector will do certain things. But if you look at where people feel left behind, it's those communities that have suffered most as a result of the conflict. It tends to be in working class Protestant and working class Catholic areas where the conflict was fought out. That's where the highest levels of poverty exist and the highest levels of economic inactivity. Our political elite have been following an economic agenda that's not addressing that."

Sophie Long makes similar observations about the need for jobs and support for different types of economic development. She says: "We should have effective policies which we don't have here at the moment in terms of how do you demonstrate to local communities, where you have levels of unemployment as pronounced as 50 years ago, where there are levels of poverty and deprivation, lack of social housing. The jobs that are coming are not reaching them.

"There are people applying for jobs who have university degrees, working in call centres. Where does that leave people who don't have university degrees? Or academic abilities? They're not even getting a chance to go for those jobs. You need to have policies where you're creating locally based initiatives, social economy initiatives, co-operatives and so forth, where people see they have a chance to be involved in the development of their communities and wider society."

Father Martin Magill is concerned about the relationship between deprivation and the attraction of paramilitary groups. "Let me go back to the [2018] Independent Reporting Commission[38] report," he says. "There was something very significant about some of its work, which focused on areas of social deprivation and paramilitary style attacks. There was such a correlation between the two. Whenever I'm talking about how we make sure young people don't get caught up with that, I want to look at it from a structural point of view, look at some of the deprivation and how we tackle that."

> "A lot of great programmes are being done and on a cross-community basis, but simply not on the scale that is required."

Senator Mark Daly makes similarly relevant points, suggesting that we are not safe from the threat of a return to violence unless we do much better in addressing deprivation and the lack of opportunity for those born into it. Referring to the report from Professors Pat Dolan and Mark Brennan with Michael Ortiz (see chapter two), Mark says it "put together a number of recommendations, in fact the vast majority of the report is about what needs to be done now in those disadvantaged communities. And a lot of the

38 First report of the Independent Reporting Commission

great programmes are there, they'd been done and they are being done on a cross-community basis but simply not on the scale that is required with the amount of money that is needed to make sure that what is termed in this report 'the Agreement generation', those who were born just before or since the Good Friday Agreement aren't radicalised, to use a term from a different conflict, and exploited by paramilitary leaders for their own ends, either in the use of republicans to achieve their aims of a border poll on a united Ireland, but then on the other side, loyalist paramilitaries wanting to maintain the status quo."

Linda Ervine believes that Northern Ireland society needs to address both deprivation and relationships in order to make progress. She says: "A lot of places in Northern Ireland have moved on and enjoy the dividends of peace. But if you're living in an interface area with a wall down the middle and still low level attacks, you didn't get that chance. They need extra help. There should be massive amounts of money and support poured in there. Their housing should be above average. They should have access to above average facilities.

"I also think, and this is very important, there should be youth work, work with the adults, that is only dealing with those areas. Not the political representatives, not somebody that lives six streets away, people who are actually living in those particular streets and dealing with the aspects of having the wall or having stones coming over. Those people should be brought together, taken away for weekends. Talked to, helped to develop their area, helped to realise that they may be living on either side of a wall, but the reality is they're facing the same problems and some of those are poverty, but when a stone comes over from somebody on say my side, over to their side and some stones from their side come over to my side, we're dealing

---

"If the peace walls are going to come down and people are going to learn to live in peace with each other, then relationships have to be made first. You can't just take the wall down and say, 'Here you are, get on with it'."

---

with the same problems. It's not Catholic youths or Protestant youths, it's *youths* who are bored, to whom this is a night's entertainment and work has to be done for those young people."

She adds: "If the walls are going to come down and people are going to learn to live in peace with each other, then relationships have to be made first. You can't just take the wall down and say, 'Here you are, get on with it'. There's a lot of intervention, a lot of money needs to be spent on skilling people. But if we have politicians coming in, or the community workers from six streets away, I don't think that's helpful. It is the actual people who are there, the actual neighbours, because that's what they are, neighbours."

Clare Bailey is another who believes we need to examine different economic structures, such as community wealth building, while reducing the environmental impact of current activities. She says: "We have to start looking at new economic models for that within community ownership, co-operatives and small scale production. There is a huge opportunity that we're going to miss in terms of having those conversations, showing people real possibility outside the narrow nationalist/unionist sense of being where people can thrive within that and it will be sustainable and fit for the future. We need to focus on that."

CHAPTER EIGHT
SHARED AND INTEGRATED EDUCATION

"The selective nature of the [Northern Ireland] post-primary educational system sees a large proportion of young people leaving school early." John FitzGerald.[39]

There is no alternative to a fundamental reform of our education sector. "I think that position of saying 'We cannot afford to keep doing what we're doing' is the baseline which has brought everybody together to say 'We actually need to talk about this'," says former Ulster Unionist Party leader Mike Nesbitt. "But it's maybe not the ideal place that I would like everybody to start from. I would rather start from a position of saying 'We are failing a lot of children in the way we are educating them'.

"I believe, although I'm from a grammar school background, that we overvalue the academic intelligence over all the other intelligences. I believe inside every child there is some spark of ability, creativity and talent. Now you may discover that in the classroom and if you do that's fine, but equally it is fine if you discover it playing a musical instrument, acting on stage, kicking a ball around a field, as long as you find it and that spark then becomes a fire or passion for life and learning and that's the sort of education system I would like to see for all our children."

"We need to seriously look at the teacher training system, which is segregated."

A similar argument is made by Peter Osborne, starting from the position of cost, social cohesion and outcomes. "We need to seriously look at things like the teacher training system, which is segregated. Can you believe it? That people who are 18 years and older, in their 20s, if you want to teach in a state or a Protestant school, you have to go to a college which is largely 90% or so Protestant. And the same on the Catholic side. You wouldn't do that in any other walk of life. How ridiculous would it be if you said, "If you want to become a doctor, you have to go to a college where you'll be trained to be a

39 https://www.irishtimes.com/business/economy/northern-ireland-s-economy-is-threatened-by-more-than-brexit-1.4009296

doctor with other Protestants" and the same, "Go to a different college if you're a Catholic, to train to be a GP as a Catholic, and you can only treat Catholics or Protestants". It's a lot of nonsense. And yet that's what we do with teachers.

"We need to take a serious look at how structurally education is managed through area planning. We need to come up with initiatives that encourage local areas where there are two, three or four schools when there should be one or two to reduce the number of schools in that area. That will save millions of pounds and our education needs that saving to go into things around teachers' assistants and the infrastructure of the schools. My son is at a school where one of the classes has to put a pot down to catch the water coming off the roof when it's raining. Yet we're wasting millions of pounds in a segregated education system. It needs really courageous big political policy decisions."

While Peter is an advocate of integrated education, he is not opposed to the building of shared education campuses. "I wouldn't be completely negative about shared education," he says. "Shared education has some valuable parts. It does bring young people together. It is more robust than just looking out windows at each other. There are activities happening that can shape and change people's perspectives. The issues I have with it are, first of all there needs to be a robust continuum of where you expect the schools and the pupils to get to, so it's not just about, 'Here's £100,000. Let's do some of these activities.' Then the money runs out and we stop doing them. They have to be moving onto a continuum where there's no going back in terms of the contact and the relationships. Otherwise, you wouldn't know what had happened when the next cadre of young people come through the education system.

"We need to take robust policy decisions about not just the continuum, but how schools move from where two become one in certain areas. We need to incentivise that. I have talked to a lot of politicians across the divide and they'll tell me they're supporters of integrated education, and that's good. But you don't see many of those politicians being public advocates for it. For many of them, they don't see the benefit to their interests or their views about life and how things should develop. We need to incentivise the schools, politicians and others to become greater advocates of changing the segregated nature of our education system.

"There's two villages a mile apart along a part of the coast in Northern Ireland. Those two villages have fewer than 250 children of primary school age. Yet those two villages a mile apart are served by four separate schools. That wouldn't happen anywhere else in these islands. How much money is spent on four schools compared to one or two? I'm sure there's hundreds of thousands of pounds of savings to be made. How do we get us a policy that says, 'If those areas reduce the number of schools from four to two, we'll keep that budget as it is.' So the total spending in those two villages on education will not change, but it will have two schools. And the £200,000 a year that the area saves will go into the now two schools.

"The local community could spend that money however they want. So there's educational underachievement? There's two or three teachers that can specifically tackle educational underachievement in those areas. There's issues around rural transport? Well, they can hire a mini bus to work in those two schools with a permanent driver. There's issues around diversity? Well, let's run a programme out of that £200,000 a year that can take P7s to places that teach them about diversity. They are worried about the transfer test, which is a problem in itself, but let's employ two teachers to work with the P6s and P7s in those two schools additional to what they would currently have to help them all through their transfer test.

"If we were to do something like that over, say, a 10-year period, suddenly that incentivises the local community and the politicians to reduce the number of schools. By reducing the number of schools, it is inevitably going to increase the sharing, but also end the segregation in education in those villages."

"I have no doubt that integrated education is fundamental to getting people to know each other, to engage with each other."

Maureen Hetherington also believes that the cost – and opportunity cost – of our divided education system creates the space to argue for a change towards a more integrated education system. She explains: "I have no doubt that integrated education is fundamental to getting people to know each other, to engage with each other. The difficulty is that we don't have the integrated society, so the social housing has to be cross community and mixed. We could highlight the cost of segregation. The majority of people out there want the best for their children, the best for the family. They want to do more than just keep surviving. They want a quality of life.

"This cost of segregation, if we can highlight that and people realise that if we can look at that and redistribute the monies elsewhere where it's really needed, people would be up for a more integrated society. The majority of people do want change. They want a better future, but it's taking that leap of faith, taking the steps towards that. Exposing the segregation for what it is, the systems and structures that are created to keep people separated, and finding ways of bringing them together."

Philip Gilliland is on this same wavelength, but warns that the complexity of the current system makes reform even more difficult. While many parents are willing for their children to attend an integrated primary school, there is a greater reluctance to do so at post-primary level. The lure of the grammar schools with an established reputation can be too great, while there are fears about the performance outcomes of some integrated secondary schools. "Actually, it's good," he adds, regarding the achievements of post-primary integrated education.

He adds: "You've got Catholic schools, you've got controlled schools or voluntary grammars, some of which are entirely one flavour only, but some of which have managed to achieve a decent mix despite their ethos. What is a decent mix? I would say anything above 20% is a pretty decent mix. As a parent of three children, two of whom have been through school with an over 20% mix, and one of them went to school that didn't and she was of the

---

"There's a *huge* difference between kids who grow up in shared schooling and kids that don't."

---

minority tribe, [I'd say] there's a *huge* difference between kids who grow up in shared schooling and kids that don't. It's the environment they're cultured in." Philip suggests those children schooled in a monocultural environment have to "unlearn" those attitudes as they enter the world of work, whereas those who went to some form of shared schooling do not.

Philip continues: "We have - I don't know what the current stat is - but something like 60,000 or 70,000 too many school places[40]. I used to be chair on a board of governors of a religiously mixed primary school. The annual subvention per child is continuing to reduce. That's just clearly nuts. Every school can't perform while we have 70,000 too many school places. Surely somebody needs to say, 'Isn't the problem that we've got 70,000 too many school places?'. Then we have to work out what is the best way to rationalise schools and when we rationalise schools guess what? We're going to actually have to mix a few of them because it's the only way to do it.

"Some situations you can rationalise within a tribe, in more country places, certainly in the west you are going to have to have multi flavoured

---

40 In 2015, schools had 70,000 surplus places. The number of surplus places has since reduced and is now reported to have fallen to 50,000 surplus places.

schools. I'm not against ethos education provided the dominant ethos understands it has to accommodate kids who aren't of that ethos. If we're being properly radical about it, we might even incentivise using something akin to anti-discrimination legislation, if a school is not able to attract an appropriate minority of its students from the non-ethos background then you get penalised financially. Put the onus on the school to get rid of the chill. There are examples of Catholic ethos schools that have happily over 20% Protestant kids and vice versa. Why shouldn't we reward those guys?"

The schooling system in the Irish Republic is beginning to change, becoming more secular, more diverse and less dominated – as it was traditionally – by the Catholic church. Fergus O'Dowd TD says that the changes are positive. "Education's a key thing," he says. "We're moving in the south. What's happening now is that if there's a new primary school wanted in an area because of population growth, the right is given to the parents to choose the school they want. I might bid - if I'm a Roman Catholic or I'm whatever religion I am, or if I'm in the community, if I'm Educate Together[41] – everybody bids and then the parents have a vote on it in a process that's away from the political system. They express their views and they're listened to and then you get the school that you want. That integration in education, male and female and regardless of one's religion, to me that's a fundamental issue. If you continue to have separate schools for separate religions, I don't think that's a good thing. Integration means you go to the same school. My view is always that you go to the school that is nearest to you."

He continues: "It's a huge change and it's very welcome, because the views of the parents are the ones that count. Everybody can bid for the school. The parents make the choice. What's happening is that primary schools are much more reflecting the changing society. I'm not making a judgement on Northern Ireland, but our society in the south is better for it. There's better integration, more awareness. I think the statistics show that County Louth's new immigrant population is twice what it is in most other counties. We have everybody here[42]. I was at a community meeting, a group here that assists and promotes integration: there were 32 different languages in the room on that day, along with the English speaking."

For Northern Ireland to become more integrated, there has to be a greater focus on integrated schools and integrated housing, argues the chief executive of the Integrated Education Fund, Tina Merron. "I think the majority of people in Northern Ireland want a shared future and a united community,"

41 https://www.educatetogether.ie/
42 Fergus is based in Drogheda, Co. Louth.

says Tina. "We need to give civil society more of a say. We need to encourage people to speak up and especially young people. And then when we do get them to speak up, we have to listen to them.

"Integrated education has been run for the last 35 years as a kind of model for wider society and it's a model that empowers parents, communities and young people. It encourages people to speak up and encourages children to look at what unites us, as opposed to what divides us. Integrated schools are safe spaces to have these discussions – children from different traditions sit side-by-side, day-by-day, learning about each other, from each other. This experience removes any fear of other traditions, different cultures and enables them to express their identity. And this has a ripple effect."

The basis for integrated education is not just about bringing pupils together from the two main traditions – the schools also attract children from other backgrounds. Integrated schools also aim to ensure children value themselves. "The ethos is about encouraging children to talk about themselves," explains Tina. "It's about them being open to discussion. It's not about burying things under the carpet. It's an opportunity for them to express themselves, to have open discussions about different issues…. It's about those from all faiths and those from no faiths at all."

Integrated schools seek to connect with local people to engage them in discussion about the future of education policy, through a programme called "Community Conversations, which empowers parents and the wider community to become involved in education, especially in area planning of education", explains Tina.

The integrated education movement wants to work more closely with elected politicians, across the spectrum. "We would encourage the politicians to go into integrated schools and have these conversations," Tina explains. "It is very important I believe for young people to vote, but young people are more interested in the social issues, health, well-being and the environment, less interested in constitutional issues. But they have to feel that their voice is being heard."

"We need these young people to start going into politics, to become politicians of the future."

Tina adds: "We need young people to enter politics. I mean if you think about it, it's 20 years since the Good Friday Agreement. So anybody under the age of 30 is less likely to be aware of, or directly impacted by, the Troubles. So what we need is for these young people to start going into politics, to become politicians of the future."

Aideen McGinley believes, though, that the expansion of integrated education in Northern Ireland faces such difficult challenges, that perhaps the effort should go into shared education, through the sharing of campuses and facilities. She explains: "Integrated education has been here a long time and it's really important, but it hasn't taken off in the way that everybody hoped it would. The complexity of our education system is ridiculous. Economic factors are now driving education in a direction that many of them were happy to sit in splendid isolation. For me, the shared education model was a really interesting one. I have grandchildren who've been beneficiaries of it. It allows people still in their space to be allowed to come out and see who else is in that space."

"The complexity of our education system is ridiculous."

There is a legitimate question, though, about the extent to which schooling children together can make up for the separation felt pre-school from the separation and sometimes isolation of communities. Greater investment in pre-school provision, such as a new generation of Sure Start projects, might address these issues and bring children together across the community divide before they start school.

Aideen says: "You've got to invest from the beginning. There's still a lot of playgroups in Northern Ireland. I know of playgroups that have been around for 40 years, they're still going strong and they're cross community in nature and that cross-community feeds back into the community hall, the fundraising, the parents knowing each other. The religious piece doesn't come into it."

As well as this, there should perhaps be fresh consideration as to whether having sixth form colleges within post-primary schools would be a better approach. Pupils and parents often complain at the lack of A level choice within sixth forms at post-primary schools. Timetabling challenges and travel arrangements make it difficult for pupils to attend other schools for specific subjects – and some schools are not fully committed to working with other colleges. Sixth form colleges that recruit across all post-primary schools would provide greater diversity both of subject choice and student composition.

Aideen is sympathetic to this view, saying that "when they get to secondary and grammar level the kids are not getting the choice of subjects. Things like the arts, languages – that's disappearing at A Level." She recognises the difficulties for schools of timetabling subjects that pupils want to take at other schools. "It's a nightmare," she says. "You've also got further education coming into play. A lot of young people want to do more technical oriented subjects." But new cross-community sixth form colleges would create greater mixing of students from different backgrounds. "Then you start to get them back together before they go into a university setting where they're in a more neutral environment."

CHAPTER NINE
PUBLIC SECTOR REFORM

"We need to take dramatic, bold policy decisions that are going to structurally change this society." Peter Osborne

Minor reforms don't cut it: Northern Ireland needs major transformation, led by fundamental change in the way our public services operate and deliver. The initial report from the new Pivotal think-tank[43] concluded that Northern Ireland has inadequate outcomes in terms of health and social care delivery; the skills base; examination passes; economic performance; carbon emissions; poverty; and community relations. The spread and scale of the weaknesses illustrate the challenges faced by government in Northern Ireland, even when it has one.

"In the years since the Agreement, we haven't taken the transformational decisions that are necessary."

"I think in 20 years since the Agreement, we haven't taken the transformational decisions that are necessary," says Peter Osborne. "We still have a society that is as segregated as it ever was. We still have new people coming through, young people reaching maturity, becoming adults, that are living in segregated housing, that go to segregated education. Because of those things, they are socialised in a way that is segregated."

Peter adds: "We need to take dramatic, bold policy decisions that are going to structurally change this society. Managing conflict and managing division is one thing, it's what the Community Relations Council does with the relatively small amount of funding that it gives out, it promotes cross community activity. What we need to do is tackle the causes of segregation and we haven't done that yet.

"I'm talking about the reconciliation agenda, about the structural change, about how we organise this society, particularly around housing and education. I'm not coming from any particular political persuasion in discussing this question, but if I was a unionist, I would want reconciliation here because I would acknowledge that reconciliation is an important part of making this place work, especially when we are all minorities in Northern Ireland now.

43 https://www.pivotalppf.org/our-work/news/8/moving-forward-putting-northern-ireland

There is no majority. We're all minorities. The only way you make this place work from a unionist perspective is to help reconcile the people in Northern Ireland so they can work together better. If you're from a nationalist or republican background, exactly the same argument applies before you can get into any substantial conversation about changing the constitutional status, or uniting the island as a whole in one political framework.

"That brings you back to reconciling the people in Northern Ireland through structural change. It is fundamentally important to both sets of people who want to either sustain the constitutional position or change the constitutional position, to get into that structural change, that change of how the society organises itself. Otherwise, you will get no movement forward. And at some point, we will go back into something that we don't want to go back into in terms of conflict. That's how important this is to reshape how this society deals with each other, to reshape the relationships that we have with each other. And that comes back to take in the big political policy decisions around housing and education."

Peter warns that the scale of change to date has been far, far too modest and slow. "We can say what we say, we can do what we do, write what we write and discuss it in the way we discuss it. Ultimately, it's up to them [elected politicians] to make the leap. The Titanic building in Belfast received 60 – six zero – million pounds of public money. A fantastic building and a great facility, but that's 60 million pounds. If the Community Relations Council were to distribute it to the core funded work that it does around reconciliation, it would take us 30 years. And the Titanic is one building amongst many that received public money on the theme of economic development.

"So, I don't think we prioritise reconciliation anywhere near as much as we should in central government. I don't think it's been resourced anywhere near as much as it should within central government, and especially not when you compare it to other things. Now, it's not about either one thing or the other, you do all of those things. But there needs to be greater prioritisation of reconciliation.

"How do you persuade politicians to do that? Well, you make the arguments, but ultimately they need to come to the same conclusions as I've come to and many others, which is that we need to put a lot more resources into it and we need to make those systemic changes to how this society works. I think many politicians are in that same place. They do understand it, but it's a huge challenge.

"When you talk about those systemic change issues, there are enormous vested interests on either side of the community that politicians need to stand up to. I suppose you're balancing out their belief in the reconciliation agenda, re-prioritising it and making the policy changes, balancing out that with the impact or influence that vested interests have on keeping the status quo as it is. Politicians need to take the courageous step and do a lot more of the challenging and a lot more of the supporting of systemic change."

Mike Nesbitt is another who believes profound change is required. In particular, he argues, Northern Ireland needs a single education system. (See Chapter Eight.)

Avila Kilmurray argues that change requires a new mindset. She explains: "Northern Ireland - any society with a lengthy violent conflict - tends to feel they're unique. As David Ervine[44] said, 'the mope syndrome', the most oppressed people ever. There is an element of that in Northern Ireland. It's probably true of any society that has been in conflict, a sort of a defensiveness, the default mode is, 'Right, they're out to get us, so what's the angle on this?', rather than saying if we're building some sort of shared society, we need to have a more open discussion about this and not take a zero sum game approach where if the republicans or if the loyalists are looking for that measure, automatically it must be bad for our community. Breaking down

---

"Could we agree some shared principles that would benefit everybody, irrespective of their identity and then work forward in terms of what policies then would flow from those principles."

---

the situation and saying, 'Could we agree some shared principles that would benefit everybody, irrespective of their identity and then work forward in terms of what policies then would flow from those principles'."

Avila also believes that the statutory sector needs to respect the community sector more as a provider of services – and not simply as a less important secondary provider that can be the first to have its funding cut. "Civil society in many ways was the backbone of society in the '70s, '80s, '90s in Northern Ireland whenever we were we were in the midst of the Troubles, but a combination of Conservative government policies plus a feeling that 'Oh, politicians are back so therefore what's the need for civil society?', has meant that a lot of the resources available for civil society, particularly from government departments, are very tied to discrete services and service provision," she says.

---

44 David Ervine was a Northern Ireland politician and leader of the Progressive Unionist Party.

"I think that non-statutories were seen as an optional extra. Obviously they weren't part of the status quo as a mainstream provider. I always argued that the benefits of civil society organisations were that they were the R&D of social provision. Any far-sighted statutory service would regard them as being very useful because they could try and do things differently, whereas if you're a health provider or whatever, it's much more difficult for you to do that."

Maureen Hetherington warns that funding cuts for community organisations plus the pressure on viability in the commercial retail sector means that many areas have lost not just services, but also places for residents to meet and socialise. To make matters worse, she argues, the design of many built communities is wrong.

She says: "There are architects exploring and researching how communities become disengaged, how community planning created these ghettos and how they've sectarianised neighbourhoods because of where they're placed. The lack of infrastructure, the lack of facilities and usually when people become angry, disenfranchised, because they do not have the necessary facilities or infrastructures for their own survival, for their own quality of life, that manifests itself in different ways.

"Community planning has a lot to answer for, where they decide to put social housing and then the consequences for the long term are negative on the people who end up there. It's usually people who are so desperate for a house, or desperate for shelter, that they're going to take what's given to them.

"Unfortunately, without the proper planning, the proper infrastructure, you can't satisfy the needs of people. I was talking to a group and they said, 'We don't even have a chemist here'. They live in a big area, it's a social housing estate. No chemist. There's no facilities for shopping. They have to travel by bus to go anywhere, so they feel dislocated from the rest of the city, disconnected as well, and there's problems with buses and different ways the infrastructure could be improved. They live in a very busy area, but it's away from a lot of the good amenities that would make their quality of life better."

The retail crisis means that in many places the provision of local commercial services is now narrowing. Maureen explains: "You look at the way Post Offices have closed everywhere, the banks, and if you don't do online banking for a lot of elderly people and people who don't have transport that's a huge problem. There's many people who are not computer literate.

"We talk about engaging civic society, but there's a huge amount of people out there at an age where they don't want to engage, or are fearful because their information has been taken or abused or sold or there are scams. People, for good reasons, decide not to engage in it. If you don't have internet, you don't have email, the chances are you're not going to be reached - because the community and voluntary sector, or pharmacies, doctors, all of those areas depend now on emails. That technology has reached the point where there's thousands of people totally disconnected because they will not use the computer, or they're fearful of their computer, or they don't know how to use it."

Another core issue is the fiscal deficit that Northern Ireland operates under, with inadequate tax income and other revenues to meet the cost of public service provision. The Pivotal think-tank notes that "The gap between public spending and tax revenue raised is £4,939 per person... the highest out of all regions"[45] (though the exact amount is subject to different calculations). "Are we as a people happy to continue to have a subvention for the next 50 years?," asks Professor Jim Dornan. "Does that make us proud? Is that good? Is that the best way to use our resources?"

Jim argues that rationalising the health service across the whole of the island of Ireland should be one element of providing better value for money and greater efficiency in the delivery of public services. All-island services such as the cancer care centre at Altnagelvin and the children's heart surgery in Dublin, provide positive examples of how we could achieve reform, says Jim.

He continues: "Ireland is a Goldilocks-sized country for health provision. We can cherry pick the best of health provision throughout the world and

---

"Our society has to take more
responsibility for its health."

---

introduce it to Ireland. The health service is a wonderful concept. Prevention is important and treatments are important. Big decisions have to be made. Our society has to take more responsibility for its health. We can't just keep abusing everything and expect an NHS to collect us at the end of the day. So somewhere between Norway and New Zealand would be my perfect health service. In New Zealand, they have a no-blame culture, so you don't have to prove that somebody's done something wrong to get help to look after your child if it's got a genetic or an acquired problem."

Jim argues that given Ireland has a population of about 6,000,000 across the island, of which 1,800,000 are in Northern Ireland, with those population numbers it would be better to provide an effective health

---

45 https://www.pivotalppf.org/cmsfiles/Publications/Moving-forward-report--web-version.pdf

service by sharing the specialisms and integrating the service across the two jurisdictions. "Although we need to work on the infrastructure," he explains. "In the west of Ireland better roads are required, linking us all up because those are the things that have the biggest influence on the health of society: access to health services.

"It's easy for people in Belfast and Dublin and maybe Cork, but those cities in the west of our island need to be connected. You know Derry, Galway, Limerick. But it is very, very manageable. The two health services *are* increasingly working together and they're full of men and women with vision. I'm positive about health going forward, but I would like to see everybody having equal access to the same health standards."

Jim argues that whatever the constitutional settlement, it makes sense to do more things on an all-island basis to improve efficiency and outcomes. "If we look at sport - football is the only sport that isn't all Ireland, everything else is. We didn't have to have constitutional change for sport to work.... Health is a perfect example of something that we can get on with now rather than wait for a potential possible change in the dispensation."

Aideen McGinley believes that Northern Ireland needs both health service reform and increased investment in the NHS. She explains: "The charity that I'm involved in buys counselling hours. The irony is we've been so successful that we're busier than we ever were, because people now know, the stigma has been removed and people now know where to come for help. The NHS mental health services are just... forget about it. The waiting lists there are just ridiculous. In fact, people are under more stress if they're there. GPs are the core. There needs to be investment in GP services."

Andrew McCracken suggests that it may make sense for a citizens' assembly, or similar, to come together to provide a public view of how we reform and structure our public services. "Creating space for the conversations and having some kind of shared picture of the society we want seems to me to be key," he says. "We allow people to come together and say, 'Okay, this is the type of education I want for my kids. This is the type of healthcare that I want to access. This is the type of leisure centre that I want to go to. This is the level of poverty I'm prepared to accept in society'. How do we move towards a society that's like that? Where we can create those conversations, we can create something that can transcend the constitutional question, but that can give us some common values and aspirations to go into it."

One of the benefits of greater all-island co-operation – without even needing to consider the constitutional question – is that there are possibilities for investment in infrastructure from three administrations, the Northern Ireland Executive, the UK government and the Irish government. Leo Varadkar, while Taoiseach, proposed investment in cross-border road, rail and university projects being jointly financed by the Irish and British governments.[46] A similar commitment formed part of the Republic's Programme for Government.[47]

"Northern Ireland needs more investment,
it needs more jobs."

Without investment and reform, cautions Fergus O'Dowd, Northern Ireland may not be functioning in a sustainable way. "Northern Ireland needs more investment, it needs more jobs," he says. "A lot of the [existing] jobs are public service jobs, excellent as the people are, but is it sustainable? If it isn't, how do you make it sustainable?" Ultimately, he suggests, it is up to nationalists to offer a vision of the future so attractive that unionists can live with it.

It should be possible to gain broad public agreement on how to modernise our society and our government, believes Ken Good. "I think what we want for the common good is big things like a health service that really works for everybody, an education system that works for everybody, jobs that are available for everybody, housing that is fair for everybody, dignity and a feeling of belonging is open to everybody. It seems self-evident to me that those are the kind of things that we are working for, if we're working for the common good. And I do believe the golden rule is an important part of this as Christians, that we're not only interested in our tribe, our people, we're interested in *all* and that must be part of civic society, working for the common good."

46 https://www.bbc.co.uk/news/uk-northern-ireland-50104226
47 https://www.greenparty.ie/wp-content/uploads/2020/06/2020-06-15-ProgrammeforGovernment_Corrected-Final-Version.pdf

CHAPTER TEN
A BILL OF RIGHTS

"A Bill of Rights is a win-win situation potentially for everyone."
Avila Kilmurray.

A Bill of Rights was mooted in the Good Friday Agreement. This stated:
"There will be safeguards to ensure that all sections of the community can participate and work together successfully in the operation of these institutions and that all sections of the community are protected, including.... the European Convention on Human Rights (ECHR) and any Bill of Rights for Northern Ireland supplementing it, which neither the Assembly nor public bodies can infringe, together with a Human Rights Commission; arrangements to provide that key decisions and legislation are proofed to ensure that they do not infringe the ECHR and any Bill of Rights for Northern Ireland... an Equality Commission to monitor a statutory obligation to promote equality of opportunity in specified areas and parity of esteem between the two main communities, and to investigate individual complaints against public bodies."

The Agreement adds:
"The Assembly may appoint a special Committee to examine and report on whether a measure or proposal for legislation is in conformity with equality requirements, including the ECHR/Bill of Rights. The Committee shall have the power to call people and papers to assist in its consideration of the matter. The Assembly shall then consider the report of the Committee and can determine the matter in accordance with the cross-community consent procedure."

It also includes:
"The Assembly will have authority to pass primary legislation for Northern Ireland in devolved areas, subject to the ECHR and any Bill of Rights for Northern Ireland supplementing it which, if the courts found to be breached, would render the relevant legislation null and void..."

More specifically the Agreement states:
"The new Northern Ireland Human Rights Commission will be invited to consult and to advise on the scope for defining, in Westminster legislation, rights supplementary to those in the European Convention on Human Rights, to reflect

the particular circumstances of Northern Ireland, drawing as appropriate on international instruments and experience. These additional rights to reflect the principles of mutual respect for the identity and ethos of both communities and parity of esteem, and - taken together with the ECHR - to constitute a Bill of Rights for Northern Ireland. Among the issues for consideration by the Commission will be: • the formulation of a general obligation on government and public bodies fully to respect, on the basis of equality of treatment, the identity and ethos of both communities in Northern Ireland; and • a clear formulation of the rights not to be discriminated against and to equality of opportunity in both the public and private sectors."

Despite this, there is as of yet no Bill of Rights for Northern Ireland. However, there has been recent progress as a result of *New Decade, New Approach*[48], which led to the establishment of an ad-hoc Assembly committee[49] to consider the creation of a Bill of Rights that is faithful to the stated intention of the 1998 Agreement. It is to include "rights supplementary to those contained in the European Convention on Human Rights (which are currently applicable) and that reflect the particular circumstances of Northern Ireland; as well as reflecting the principles of mutual respect for the identity and ethos of both communities and parity of esteem," said NDNA.

Several of our interviewees expressed serious unhappiness about the slow progress, believing this represents a breach of the Good Friday Agreement and the goodwill that created it. What is more, argues Avila Kilmurray, the questions about a Bill of Rights have been reduced to an issue of how they affect each of the main traditional communities – rather than considering whether in itself it would be a good thing.

"Our politics has become so narrowed by the constitutional division that things like a Bill of Rights became a victim of the unionist/nationalist divide."

She observes: "Our politics has become so narrowed by the constitutional division that things like a Bill of Rights became a victim of the unionist/nationalist divide, without people actually getting a chance to

48 https://assets.publishing.service.gov.uk/government/uploads/system/uploads/attachment_data/file/856998/2020-01-08_a_new_decade__a_new_approach.pdf
49 http://www.niassembly.gov.uk/assembly-business/committees/2017-2022/ad-hoc-committee-on-a-bill-of-rights/

say, 'Well, what does that mean for me and my community?'. Listening to someone like Albie Sachs[50] talking about the Bill of Rights in South Africa, a Bill of Rights is a win-win situation potentially for everyone. But here it became 'Oh, a Bill of Rights must be a republican demand, so therefore it's not for us'. When I was involved in social justice funding for the Community Foundation back in 2004/2005, when the Bill of Rights consultations were happening, we were funding the Evangelical Alliance[51] to look at a biblical analysis of human rights. We were funding a lot of loyalist communities who said 'What we want to see is socio-economic rights'. And yet the unionist parties said, 'Oh no, no, no, we can't have socio-economic rights in it. This has to be purely on civil liberties or issues in relation to the Troubles'."

Conal McFeely believes that social and economic concerns should sit at the heart of a Bill of Rights for Northern Ireland. He explains: "If we look at the situation where we are today, we have a situation that if people had implemented the Good Friday Agreement in terms of a Bill of Rights, addressing inequality in economic investment, targeting the most marginalised communities within our societies be they within working class communities - be they loyalist, be they republican, be they nationalist, be they unionist - we could have seen greater movement. It is a great disappointment that within that framework was a Civic Forum concept that the first thing that our politicians did was throw out.

> "If we had policies that addressed economic disadvantage, social disadvantage, educational disadvantage and ensured that was applying right across all those communities, then civic society would be strengthened."

"You have a situation now where people say, 'How do we create a more proactive civic society?'. If we had a proactive civic society, if we had an effective Bill of Rights, if we had policies that addressed economic disadvantage, social disadvantage, educational disadvantage and ensured that was applying right across all those communities, then civic society would be strengthened. We would have a more cohesive society and we could have built and strengthened our peace."

He adds: "People need to go back to basics and ask themselves, why was the Good Friday Agreement brought about? People wanted an end

---

50 Albie Sachs was an anti-apartheid activist who became a judge in post-apartheid South Africa.
51 The Evangelical Alliance is a Christian pressure group.

to conflict. It's much wider than that. A lot of people who voted for the Good Friday Agreement said 'Let's look at the reasons and the history that give rise to conflict'. We need to create a framework that would create a situation where we had a society that was a shared society, where people's rights were respected, equality for all. We need a Bill of Rights that looks at the economic, educational, social needs of people."

"The strengthening of any society has to be based
on a rights-based agenda."

This view is shared by Maeve McLaughlin, a former Sinn Féin MLA and now the manager of the Derry Model project. She says: "The strengthening of any society has to be based on a rights-based agenda. I believe that if the legislative framework isn't in place to protect, support, give redress to residents, to people in society, that we're missing a trick. Rights have to be looked at in the broadest possible way.

"We, I think for too long, looked at rights simply as human rights. The debate onus was on the positive things around development of a Bill of Rights, understanding that rights are social, they're economic, but they have to be enshrined in law and I think that whilst we can have all the engagements if you like across sections of society, that if we don't have that legislative framework [it means nothing]….

"My overview of the conflict was about injustice. Whilst I recognise that a lot of very important engagements and projects and initiatives took place across what was perceived as both communities, if that rights-based agenda wasn't addressed, people simply went into their own communities. Certainly as a republican growing up in the Bogside, that sense of 'I don't have redress. I don't have protection in law', was very strong for me. So to strengthen civic society we have to do it on the basis of that framework, which is the broadest possible rights-based agenda that we can move towards."

CHAPTER ELEVEN
THE ROLE OF THE MEDIA

*"What is the purpose of trying to start discussion and debate if all
we're going to do is poke people in the eye with a stick?"*
Máirtín Ó Muilleoir.

What is the role of the media in a post-conflict society? There is a new
consideration within parts of the media about what is termed 'peace
journalism'. But what does this mean and what does it represent? To what
extent do journalists have a responsibility to consider the impact of our
actions? Should thye refuse to name a person in a story if, by doing so,
they are putting lives at risk? Should they fail to report a crime involving
paramilitaries if it puts the peace process at risk? Or should they report the
facts, while doing so in a way that is accurate and objective, while avoiding
inflaming a situation? But is this possible?

Then again, do parts of the media gain ratings or sales by providing an
outlet for the most base comments, stoking division?

These are all matters of concern raised by interviewees.

Ken Good observes: "If it's not too rude to say it, I would like to see
our politicians speaking *less* or at least be reported less, and for Civic Forum
people to be speaking more, or to be quoted more, or to be asked more."
Asked if he was making a specific point about the aggressive style of Radio
Ulster presenter Stephen Nolan, Ken responds: "I think the adversarial way
in which these things are set up is counterproductive. It has to be adversarial
for his - I won't personalise it - but for those kinds of shows to work there
has to be cut and thrust and 'I'm against you and I'm strongly against you'.
No consensus is possible in the adversarial format that's devised. So that's not
the way forward for me."

> "It is a truism that you learn more more by
> listening, not by talking."

Stephen Nolan was named specifically by Sinn Féin's then MLA Máirtín
Ó Muilleoir. He observes: "I think we could start by listening. It is a truism
that you learn more, I invariably learn more by listening not by talking. I

don't have all the answers in this but I have been for 30 years of political activity a big believer in building community. That's the phrase I use really for developing and working for the common good.

"That has to be to the fore in our mind if we are going to adopt any strategies, whether around economic development, whether around providing an adequate health service for our people, focusing on education, building healthy, prosperous societies. I think we have to be focused on the common good. How do we do that in this often divided society: I think the tone and timbre of the debate has to be respectful, we have to find ways of not feeding the ratings monster.

"We have to find ways of not sectarianising discussion, which has issues of sectarian elements in it, we have to find ways not always to try and have a race to the bottom in terms of the dialogue and debate and turn it into a rant.

"I speak to you this morning after having been on the Nolan Live [TV] show last night. I have huge respect for Stephen Nolan. I think he is the pre-eminent broadcaster on the island, certainly in the north of the island, but as he knows, there are a lot of angry people out there and he has to find a way to get the balance between making those people angrier and instead of that, trying to find a way for angry people to express, to emote, to vent – if necessary – but what is the purpose of us as a society in trying to start discussion and debate that you're talking about if actually all we're going to do is poke people in the eye with a stick or make people a wee bit more polarised?

"I was the mayor of Belfast... when I first joined the council in 1987 I wore a flak jacket, we weren't allowed to speak. I was put out by the RUC after ten minutes on my first night. We had orange juice thrown over us, we fought, physically fought, DUP councillors and so on and so forth. And now it's a beacon of unity and collegial relations and therefore being mayor was easy until someone mentioned the past. And once the past was mentioned it was almost as if you entered a different, a parallel universe where the tone of the debate sharpened, the unwillingness to countenance any other view was to the fore, that the bitterness came, I suppose oozed out on all sides because as Seamus Heaney said, people hurt and get hard.

"So, for me, if we are going to try and find ways to build a stronger civic society, we're going to have to find ways to engage in a frank debate because there's no sense a lot of blushing violets, shrinking violets saying, 'We're not going to talk about this and talk about that'. So we need to find a safe space in which to do that."

Sophie Long points out that media outlets – and their readers and listeners

– are less interested in the positive stories of progress than they are of disaster and tragedy. She relates the lack of coverage of cross-community work done by women's groups, that are embedding reconciliation. "They had built friendships over the years and had been trying to do things around the interface. That got drowned out because media outlets here focus on stuff that's related to conflict. Bomb scares get headlines. The old digital editor of the *Belfast Telegraph* said at an event a couple of years ago, the only time he'd ever sold out of a paper when it wasn't to do with violence was when he had Rory McIlroy on the cover. So you have to understand how the media operate."

But Sophie welcomes efforts to ensure that journalists behave ethically, avoiding upsetting victims, for example. She says: "That's why it was good to see the guidelines for the media when reporting on victims, to tell people on certain anniversaries, 'Don't phone up people and ask for a photo of them looking distressed'. They are not these bank accounts full of stories that you can tap whenever you need something. And victims have loads of other aspects to their identity and sometimes they're happy to share their story for a certain purpose and sometimes they maybe just want to be left alone, but the media here, some of them have a bit of a weird obsession with sadness and trauma. I suppose it sells papers."

Maureen Hetherington is concerned, though, at the way social media operates – and this, of course, is not subject to the regulation imposed on traditional print and broadcast media. Many social media participants even ignore legal concerns such as libel, contempt of court and intimidation.

> "There has to be ways in which we mitigate the use of social media and get people back into conversations with each other."

Maureen says: "It surprises me how many people are so disconnected almost from reality because of the introduction of social media and apps and different ways of communicating. They're overwhelmed by the amount of stuff that's put into their brains and into society. I think that it has been very damaging, particularly for young people who have an expectation of life and what life should be for them and disappointment whenever it doesn't come up to reality, doesn't come up to the fantasy world that they create through their social media.

"There has to be ways in which we mitigate the use of social media and get people back into conversations with each other. It's about quality time. I don't think that's impossible to achieve. The way we do things like talking at people and being quite negative - we have to make everything very attractive for people to re-engage. And that depends on how we engage. What is it that people are interested in? And it has to be based on self-interests.

"What's in their interests? Better health, wellbeing, particularly mental health. To make civil society move forward, to progress, we have to encourage them to look at a different way of being, with communicating with each other. The negativity around the news and what we hear gets us overwhelmed every day. There has to be a balance about how much they can take in, because it does become overwhelming.

"Whenever you try to encourage people to think of the common good you can get a change in attitude and mindsets."

"It's about parents looking at young people and trying to encourage different ways of being with each other, opening up different ways of communicating and engaging with people at what their self-interests are. Ultimately, whenever you try to encourage people to think of the common good you can get a change in attitude and mindsets. People are like sheep, they follow and it's a way of re-engaging in a different way that values them. It's surprising how many people have no self-worth. The people we work with at the grassroots, they don't feel they've got anything to say, or that it's worth saying. You wonder what's happening in schools. It might be churning out excellence and academia, but what's it doing to young people and how are young people allowed to engage in so much social media that turns back on them as to how they see themselves and their world view and how negative and overwhelming it is."

Maureen concedes that social media can be positive. "There's always a balance to be struck," she agrees. "If you look at the social media around #MeToo, the amount of trolls and negativity and the *backlash* for many people who spoke out was devastating for a lot of people. You get that constantly where social media will gather a range of diverse opinions, but some are so negative that no matter how good or well intended messages are, you have the kickback.

"If you look at what Donald Trump is doing and the tweets that he's putting out and then the response to that. The kickback can be far more damaging. We should be aware of what's happening in the world. We are a global village and it's really important that we are connected because we can't be ourselves alone. We're part of a huge planet. The environment has to be looked after. We have to look after ourselves: the French philosopher says, 'When I look at you, I am responsible for you'.[52] So we all have that responsibility of how we see each other as neighbours, brothers, sisters. Whenever it gets overwhelming people will switch off, but then that negativity is easy to exploit and manipulate people to think in a particular way. You ultimately have the altruistic side, but you've also got the rise of the very right wing fundamentalism that comes out directly as a result of that negative social media."

She continues: "I support the Peter Tatchell Foundation[53]. Despite the awful things that have happened to that man he has been able to promote ways in which countries are doing good work with regards to the gay and lesbian community. We can see how lucky we are that we live in this society, but also the desperate needs that have to be addressed in other countries. That fight for good can trump the negativity. Up to a point, the #MeToo campaign encouraged women to come out and speak out which is brilliant, but then for the women that did speak out there is a huge kickback and a lot of negativity that came with that. How do you choose your battles, because it's never straightforward. It's long, drawn out and you can suffer for a long, long time after it whenever you put things on social media."

"You need to find ways of coming up with new systems of engagement."

Conal McFeely is more positive about how social media can be made to work for the benefit of the community sector and for promoting healing and reconciliation. (One of Rath Mor's projects is the Hive Studios, a digital community communications studio.[54]) Conal argues: "You need to find ways of coming up with new systems of engagement. We can deal with that through creative arts, through different approaches, using different media tools. We have to find ways to ensure that voice is given to those voices that have previously been denied or silenced, or quite deliberately forgotten about. I would cite an example which has happened here at Creggan Enterprises where we felt that we had to give voice to women.

---

52 Emmanuel Levinas, see http://www.jcrelations.net/
Levinas+and+the+Other+Side+of+Theology.2234.0.html?L=3.
53 The Peter Tatchell Foundation is a human rights charity, established by gay rights campaigner Peter Tatchell.
54 http://hivestudio.org/about/

"The *Unheard Voices* programme[55] we're doing here where people are talking about the past, they talk about the people who lost their lives, we wanted to talk about the people who had to carry on after those lives were lost. What was the impact on women? What was the impact on families? As a result, that brought people from right across the divide here to talk about the impact of violence. That is dealing with the past.

"The vast majority of people who want to deal with the past just want to know what happened, why it happened, they want to know the context and so forth. That's why... we shouldn't be making the mistakes of the past. The mistakes of the past came as a result of failure of political governance, the failure of bringing in security measures that don't work. And in that sort of situation we need to find ways of creating new roots of activity and ways of doing things and that's what I would simply say is one way and means of doing it."

Drama can also play an important role in healing society – though it must be considered carefully to ensure it does not have the opposite effect. Derry's Playhouse Theatre in partnership with the Holywell Trust, the Thomas d'Arcy McGee Foundation and Queen's University Belfast have been engaged in a Peace Building Academy, with finance from the European Union's Peace Programme.[56] This produces performances based on events in the Troubles, including stage presentations by individuals explaining their personal and family experiences. Participants come from various backgrounds, including former members of the RUC, paramilitary groups and victims. The aim is to promote mutual understanding.

There are clearly examples of different types of media engaging consciously in social healing, while others are focused on hard news reporting, while apparently rejecting the idea that they have a role in bringing society together. It is perhaps for society as a whole, rather than just media participants, to discuss how media should operate and what responsibilities they have.

---

55 https://www.northernslant.com/unheard-voices/
56 https://keep.eu/projects/20037/

CHAPTER TWELVE
THE FUTURE

"Our problem at the moment is we don't know where we're going."
Denis Bradley.

We don't spend anything like as much time thinking about the future as we do about the past, points out Avila Kilmurray. She argues we need to move beyond this by adopting "long term visioning". However, she argues, we should not be scared of implementing the Good Friday Agreement's commitment to being willing to discuss the constitutional arrangements and moving towards a referendum on possible Irish unity.

Avila says: "It has been wrong to say that the republican/nationalist call for a border poll and a united Ireland is at odds with reconciliation. That then is privileging one constitutional view over another. It is valid to have that conversation. There is a real need for a parallel discussion within unionism/loyalism, rather than just saying, 'No surrender, ourselves alone' to saying, 'Where would we be in 20 years' time?'. In order not to be in a situation where that broader community feel that they're being left with no alternatives, they start having internal conversations with a range of options so they can have an input into positively framing where they want to go.

"In terms of a border poll, which clearly is in the Good Friday/Belfast Agreement, the worst thing is winners and losers syndrome. It may be hard to escape that, but if we use the time prior to fashioning questions, to again start talking to one another about a range of options that are not as stark as a united Ireland in the morning, run from Dublin, or remain in the UK, run from London.

"The worst thing is winners and losers syndrome."

"[That] could be around regionalism, devolution. Commonwealth membership has been put on the table. Then there is the added complication of relations with the European Union. So you're moving towards a 'preferendum'. Part of that conversation should be driven from the Republic, because they've got a 100 year old system that is operating - how satisfactory is another question, but it actually operates. Many from the Republic [might say], 'That would be a headache bringing them in'.

She adds: "There is a danger that politicians will dub anybody who tries to have the conversation as a traitor. However, we've seen people like Peter

Robinson sort of saying, 'Look, we need to start looking forward'. So we have people who have long experience say, 'We're in danger of digging ourselves into a hole here if we aren't prepared to engage in long term visioning'."

Should we be asking, not what do we want, but what we would accept, wonders Avila. "A lot of it is the way we frame that consensus. A lot of opinion polling coming up to the Good Friday Agreement was around, 'What do you want?'. There was one poll carried out by academics in Queen's, funded by the Rowntree Foundation, which said, 'What are you prepared to settle for?', with totally different results. So how you frame that conversation in such a way that you're not pushing the 'all or nothing', which a lot of our politics do, then I think you'll have more of a chance of trying to look again at what would be a win-win situation."

But Ken Good argues that it impossible to make progress on the constitutional question unless there is an absence of politically-linked violence, plus genuine commitment to make the current institutions work. He says: "The first requirement for the debate to take place openly is to have a complete end to violence. That needs to be removed from the debate and discussion. The whole discussion is coloured if violence is still an option, or a weapon, or a threat. Now that sounds idealistic, but it's true." Ken's second requirement was the restoration of the power-sharing institutions that has been achieved since the interview. "History has shown it's counterproductive to have a vacuum there," he observes.

"Thirdly, the tone needs to be set in which the debate can happen fairly and honestly and securely. I think the political agreement that we have at the moment, it's like a backstop for the discussions to happen and they could with these other requirements that I've outlined, the discussions could happen then more securely.

"But what is thrown into the mix is Brexit and the irony probably now is that the union is at threat more because of Brexit and Scotland than anything. Scotland could well be the partner to break the union.... That's highly ironic, but that could be lead us into a whole new environment about what does the union mean for Northern Ireland? We're in unknown and uncharted territories."

Progress "means 'not doing what we are doing at the moment," suggests Anthony Russell. "We have two blocks intent on maximizing the power of that ethnicity. I suppose that's inevitable. We saw that when Sinn Féin came within twelve hundred votes of the unionist parties. The next election there were tens of thousands between the two. People were not voting on DUP economic policy. They weren't voting on Sinn Féin economic policy. They were voting to the drumbeat and that comes back to what I was trying to say, dealing with that is fundamental to any solution. Having said that, I know from talking to the Protestant community, talking to unionists, that they are aware underneath the 'no surrender' façade - which appears to be their state about Brexit - they are aware of the demographic changes, of the geographical changes and I think they are much more prepared to talk and to compromise and to listen and ask to be listened to than they ever were previously."

For us to have a reasonable conversation about the future constitutional arrangements we need both clarity about what we are potentially stepping into, but also the honesty to say about the past that we must accept there are different versions of history – and about what was right and wrong, stresses Peter Sheridan.

"I have said it in previous discussions with people like Martin McGuinness that I was willing to accept that he had a story for the last 30 or 35 years," says Peter. "I wasn't going to say that I agreed with it, or agreed with all aspects of it, or that I accepted it in its totality, but I was willing to accept it was his story. On one condition. That he accepted that I had an understanding of the last 35 years and likewise he didn't have to agree with it, agree with all the sentiment, or accept it was right. But what he would do is accept that it was my story.

"I think once you can get people to think in that way then you have the possibility of being able to look to the future. The way we are doing it now - going back over 40 years, trying to decide who's right and who's wrong in every instance - and we will still not agree. People will still have a viewpoint of what they saw at a particular time and a lot of people's knowledge has now been coloured by what they've read, what they've seen since the event. I have examples in my last role where people thought they had seen something, but it turned out it was something they had read in more recent years. So what you do is you tell your story and then when you tell it again you add in something else you've learned and you continue at that stage. So I just think we are approaching this in a way we will never resolve it and it will continue to be an ongoing sore."

He adds that "the first thing we have to do is to not do what we're doing now at the minute, which is saying we have to have a border poll. A border poll now to me it's a bit like what people did in Brexit. Let's have a border poll, decide yes or no and then we'll decide what it looks like.

"We have not had the conversation with people in Cork to say, 'What might this mean for the Irish flag? What might this mean for the Irish national anthem?'. Never mind all of the other arrangements in terms of how would you end up with a policing environment, a health environment, education environment... the notion that you have this simplistic position where you make a quick decision on something as complex as that and decide, 'Now we'll fix it altogether'. Is it the view that in that quick decision that the result is we simply bolt on? If the decision was we're moving to a united Ireland, to say that had happened at the border poll, that we simply bolt on 750,000 Protestants and we expect them to stand for the national anthem and the Irish flag?

"If you want to convince people that that's where we should go then let's tell everybody what it looks like. Let's thrash out those details. And if that takes five years, it takes 10 years, so be it. It is absolutely important to have that debate and that conversation but to test out all of those things now and not simply a yes or no vote, and then we'll decide how we get on with it.

"What our society also needs to do is perhaps worry less about irritating people who lose out in a process of engagement – that is normal in a process of democracy to have winners and losers. Both sides need to accept this."

Denis Bradley is frustrated at where we find ourselves at present. "Our problem at the moment is we don't know where we're going," he says. "We don't know where we're going at the moment, we may have very strong ideas of where we may go in the future and where we should go in the future. Just in this moment in time, it's not very clear. There is a time in politics to sit back and engage in a conversation knowing that it is not the time to strike, not the time to make anything really happen, that you just have to be patient, that you have to realise that this is a change. If you were to try to force that situation at this moment in time, it's incredibly difficult and maybe even impossible because all of the politics will say, 'Ah yes, but...' and that 'but' will keep you outside that door or outside that engagement for a period of time at least. How long that period is, is questionable.

"Brexit is such a revolutionary thing that it's in the throes of its dynamics and until its dynamics at least comes to earth somewhere and settles down and there's a greater clarity, it is going to be nigh impossible to construct anything else in any of the countries that we're talking about and what I mean by that is Ireland, Scotland, not so much Wales, and England itself. Those things are so disrupted and are going to be for the next period of time that it is very hard to know what we can do except I suppose observe to a degree, engage to a degree in which is practical and realise that it is going to be very frustrating for a period of time."

Denis continues: "Something very important happened and has not received the attention it should have. And that is that the Europeans and the Irish, but particularly the Europeans, have said if there is a no deal [Brexit] we will still have to deal with the Northern Ireland situation. That's a *massive* movement from where situations were at. My argument was that I didn't think that they're ever, ever, ever could be a border in Ireland again.

"And anyway all the border structures would be within green territory. What I mean by 'green territory' is from here [in Derry] to Dundalk is basically, with a few exceptions, a few pockets, it's basically a nationalist homeland. So to think that you could [construct a physical border] is [like] thinking that you can put the cavalry of the old western films out into a fort somewhere and that the Apaches will stand off. The Apaches won't have to stand off because the locals just won't let it happen. I also think it's an understanding that we're different from Scotland, who will have their own fight. I think they will start calling for their second referendum. The fascinating thing about Brexit is that it was an English construct and it is going to leave England incredibly unsettled for a long period of time. Now whether that's five years or 10 years or a generation, I do not know.

"The real question for us is, can we move beyond that unsettlement in England, to actually engage in a real and honest and radical engagement in this island?... What we need is an all-island forum. What we need is conversations to start. What we need is engagement from all the different parts of this island. But I say that almost out of desperation.... I see unionism's propensity to go back in on itself and at difficult moments not to engage - I can understand why this is. They come from a position that nationalism can lose 20 times or 40 times. Unionism can only lose once. They will become incredibly defensive.

"My contact with loyalism over the last 20 years has been substantial and they have been very angry with the DUP because they feel betrayed by the DUP and they feel that the DUP looks down their nose at them. And they are much less willing to be radicalised into, 'We will create havoc on the streets if we lose the precious union or the precious union's under threat'. But then again, the people I'm talking to are kind of a bit like myself, getting old."

Denis accepts that there are many shades of loyalism and unionism, as well as big splits between Sinn Féin and what might be termed traditional constitutional republicanism. "Sinn Féin are the strong party on the nationalist / republican side in Ireland around the referendum, around the border poll. And they're the ones who are calling for it.

"The southern government and the southern parties are saying this is crazy, it's not the right time, not the right way to go about it. So there's tension in there. Of course it's the wrong time and it's simplistic and crude and wrong to have a border poll now which would say if there's one more voter for a united Ireland then that is it. That's as crude as you can get. The difficulty is that if you take that off the table I'm not convinced unionism will move at all, it will stay within its own narrow ground. It won't move out into engagement. So in fact I think that the border poll, or the possibility of a border poll, at least challenges unionism. Peter Robinson was prepared to look at that and trying to make his people ready for that. One of my disappointments is that that hasn't been followed through much by many people within unionism. Robinson seemed to be this lone voice.

"I think it was [SDLP leader] Colum Eastwood who said it's very hard to have a conversation with people who don't want to talk to you. Is there anybody, are there institutions, is there civic society within unionism, which is prepared to talk? Until that happens it's very hard to judge which would be the best type of forum, would it be better at a local level, would it be better at an all-Ireland level, would it be better if the two governments agreed to it, would it be better?

"Are there any church people saying anything? Are there any non-politicians saying anything? The Ulster Unionists may talk about Brexit, but will they talk about anything beyond that? The commercial people, the industrial people will talk about Brexit, but that's safe because what they're saying is, 'This is bad for our economy'. I have friends who say the politicians need to be taken out of this. What we really need to do here is work on the economics and the social change and I can see that argument and I can understand it and I'm caught between 'Is that the best place to go into safe territory?', or 'Does unionism need [to be] challenged, really challenged to say you have a responsibility here too?'"

But what will happen with unionism showing new signs of internal tension over varying attitudes to the EU? "Will we get those 20% or 30% who were anti-Brexit within the unionist community to begin to speak into this chaos that we're now living with, or will they retrench and not speak and just hold schtum?," asks Denis. "I don't know and I'm fascinated by that. I had one very interesting conversation with four elderly members of Presbyterian congregations within the heartlands of unionism. I pressed them on this and the initial thing was, 'A lot of our people don't talk about it', but the most hardline of the four said, 'I would say that there is a lessening of attachment to the union'. There is not a lot of discussion around the future, but they would recognise the lessening of attachment to the union."

Peter Sheridan believes we have reached the point where we should worry less about upsetting those parts of the Northern Irish population who lose the argument. "You are going to upset people. It's not possible to have it without upsetting someone. I think your question is how we can make progress on that anyway. At this point it's like a spectrum. You don't want to crowd one thing with another. At this point in time the focus should be on let's have our self-government here and get it going and let that self-government be supported, well supported, and well resourced by citizens in civil society, and then people can have that dialogue. That can become a mechanism for moving forward. I think to just jump in now is difficult and dangerous."

Linda Ervine accepts that Brexit has shifted opinion on Irish unity amongst many people, including within the unionist community. "There does seem to be a change," she says. "It's a small change, it's a gradual change, I suppose it's Brexit and it's the Good Friday Agreement and people changing allegiance and exploring new ideas. I don't think it's helpful to say that we can't talk about it. That's pointless and will lead us into a situation where if change does come - which may or may not happen, because that's going to be up to the people of Northern Ireland - then it will be a shock and could then bring us back to war.

"I feel things are changing and not just in Northern Ireland. Things are changing in the UK. We've seen movement in Scotland where there was a referendum which didn't end up in an independent Scotland, but that is a change that has a possibility and might come. If I could personally wave my magic wand, I would like to see a federation of islands. The identity issue with an all Ireland isn't an issue for me. The issue for me would be the practical outcomes, the National Health [Service]. I like the National Health [Service], I like being British, I like enjoying the British way of life.

"For me, if a constitutional change has to come, I want to keep very close links with the rest of the UK and I wonder is there some way that a new discussion could be opened up. At the minute the only discussion we seem to have is UK or all Ireland. There doesn't seem to be a recognition, could we not have an all-Ireland that would be within a close-knit British Isles, is that not a possibility? Why could that not happen and I'm not talking about Ireland coming back into the Commonwealth, but it would bring Ireland into closer links with other countries within the UK. Could that not open up a new discussion?"

The important principle, suggests Linda, is to be willing to engage in the conversation without fear. "This idea that if you talk about it, it's going happen. No, if you talk about it, that's just talking about possibilities. Is it that things stay the same or that things could stay the same but be tweaked? But, if the population is changing and we know that the nationalist community is rising, which again doesn't necessarily mean that people will automatically vote for a UI, it doesn't automatically mean that people from the unionist community are going to vote for the UK either, but it's just opening up the discussions especially now because of Brexit.

"I have been surprised at some of the people from the unionist community who have started to say, 'Well actually, I would be in favour of going into Ireland'. So there is a change in mindset and the only way we can respectfully deal with that and acknowledge that is by giving people space to talk without attacking them. One of the big issues in Northern Ireland is if people say something different and people they see as stepping out of line, they're not talking the party line, all of a sudden they're a Lundy, they're a traitor. But you're not a Lundy or a traitor, you've got a different point of view which may or may not be a popular point of view. I feel one of the strengths about being part of the UK is a democracy that allows you to express a different point of view."

But we must avoid repeating the mistakes of the Brexit referendum, believes Linda. "One of the issues with Brexit is that there was a lot of misinformation. They voted on very narrow information on a very complex topic. I didn't vote because I felt I couldn't make an educated vote. I didn't know which way to vote because I couldn't understand what I was voting for, what I was going to vote for, what I was going to vote against. I didn't want to stay in Europe, didn't want to come out of Europe. I regret now that I didn't vote to stay, but at the time I really listened to the arguments and I rejected the racist ones, but I wasn't sure was Europe a good thing. It went from being the European Union into something different, this kind of state that had a lot of corruption in it, but I wasn't sure that I wanted to come out either. I just couldn't make the call."

Mark Daly also says that we must avoid again having a referendum, in which we vote first and find out what it means after. He argues that "we have to look at the next steps forward in terms of the future generations. And that is the challenge as a result of Brexit as well having the conversation about what is the best for the people of Northern Ireland about the future of Northern Ireland, having the debate between unionism and nationalism about is it better to stay in the United Kingdom or is it better to be in a united Ireland? But the problem, as we've seen with Brexit, is logic doesn't always come to the fore and identity is a very important issue. You have to address people's fears and concerns and that's one of the other pieces of work I'm looking at at the moment, but it's really about putting the work in place now."

Mark accepts that Brexit has inflamed community differences within Northern Ireland, but also says we should not be unduly influenced by the fear of what that signifies. "I suppose people are pointing to that, but in reality the tensions are there and what some people are looking for is the excuse. And we saw that with the flags protest in 2012/13 where young people were holding banners, people who weren't born during the Troubles and were very young during the Troubles, they were holding banners saying, 'We will not be the generation to fail Ulster'. And that was before Brexit. So you know that's a concern in the run up to any future border poll.

"And the thing is in reality there's going to be a referendum on a united Ireland. The question is when. And how it's conducted. And that is a great lesson in policy neglect because I was in Belfast when Raymond McCourt[57] took the secretary of state to court seeking the secretary of state to come up with a policy on how a referendum on a united Ireland would be called. And the secretary of state was not forced to come up with a policy because of what the judge said.

"What ultimately happened in that court case was that Justice Girvin said, 'I cannot force her to come up with a policy, even though it would be prudent for her to have one and it may be prudent', but he said it, I imagine, as a combination of election results, opinion polls, and the problem with that is that opinion polls are showing the event of a hard border due to Brexit, the majority would vote for a united Ireland. And the election results in 2017 show that the majority of people did not vote for pro-union candidates. Now that's People Before Profit, Alliance, Sinn Féin and SDLP and the Greens. So that's not decisive.

"But at some stage it will be decisive. The predictions are somewhere between 2023/24 and 2029. Ten years max. And knowing all these facts, what are the governments doing, the Irish government, the British government, with the assistance of the European Union and the United States, going to prepare for that reality, that there is going to be a referendum. And people will have their views obviously. I want to see a united Ireland but all we have to do is learn those lessons of the past, learn the lessons of Brexit, you sit

---

57 Raymond McCourt is a victims campaigner and human rights activist.

down, you engage with people, you talk about their fears and concerns. You address their grievances and then you move forward. So the debate that needs to happen is the debate between people with ideas... And that is a debate about the day-to-day issues like housing, health, education, opportunity.

"When you have those debates and ideas - obviously also addressing people's concerns - that's all done under the umbrella of the Good Friday Agreement. People may not understand this but under any united Ireland, Stormont remains... Issues of the Commonwealth and flags and anthems, statues and issues of identity all have to be addressed. But that needs to be done now in the build-up. It cannot be done in the 12 months before a referendum. That's simply too late."

But, Mark adds, we need clarity over how a referendum would be conducted. "One of the things in that court case, and the most disturbing thing in that court case, outside of the fact that the secretary of state could call a border poll at any moment, but that's unlikely, it's more likely the secretary of state would be *forced* to call a referendum by being taken to court and it going all the way to the Supreme Court and a judge is saying, 'Well, the evidence is there and therefore you must call a border poll'. You do not want a border poll caused by protests and people on the streets protesting for a referendum being called... because the simple fact is there is no policy, nobody knows the grounds on which a referendum will be called.

"But what I must mention is that not only does the Secretary of State decide when the border poll gets called, but also the Secretary of State decides who gets to vote and in Northern Ireland that is disastrous given the context of gerrymandering and vote rigging that happened in the past. And the reason that is of concern is if you took the Scottish independence referendum they decided that everybody on the local election register got the vote and they obviously had it from 16 and up which suited the independent side because young people were more in favour of Scottish independence.

"But what they found is when they did the exit polls, the people who were from, we all know it was lost by 45/55, but people from elsewhere in the UK voted against Scottish independence by 75%. People from outside of the UK, EU citizens who were allowed to vote, voted against it 57%. But people from Scotland who were born in Scotland voted by a margin of 49/51. So people who were Scottish voted by just a margin of 1%, so a 1.1% swing and you're home and hosed.

"If you take that into a Northern Ireland context, you can decide the outcome. The Secretary of State could decide the outcome of the referendum long before any vote is cast because if the 16 year olds are allowed a vote that obviously favours one community, if it's 18 year olds, it affects a community. If it's British passport holders, British and Irish passport holders, British, Irish and European passport holders, you have different outcomes depending on that. So there is another court case. So without that policy being put in place now, all you're going to have is chaos in the run up to referenda, you're going to have court case after court case where the Secretary of State will come up with, 'Here are the parameters for the voter register for the referendum'. Guaranteed to be taken to court by one side or the other.

"That's the work that needs to be done now because if you don't do that work now you are adding fuel to a tense situation and then all it needs is a spark. And it doesn't have to be that way. Because that's the job of politics, the job of politics is to plan and prepare. No one ever got a statue put up to them because they prevented a war. Nobody. But this is all highly foreseeable. All the outcomes that we're talking about are highly foreseeable, very predictable, some are very likely. So therefore that requires government to act."

It is important, believes Mark, to have as much clarity as soon as possible over how and when a referendum would be conducted. "It becomes far too tense and that's where it's like you need to establish those rules and parameters well in advance but also address people's fears and concerns. That's a very important issue. So the issue of land ownership in Northern Ireland and I've met members of the unionist community who think the land is going to be taken off them. I said to them, 'Who do you think we're going to give it to?'. You know? But there was intimidation in the '20s, there was intimidation in the '70s and '80s and when I say 'intimidation', farmers were killed in the hope that their families would sell the land. That's a reality. It wasn't widespread, but it happened. And that fear needs to be addressed. So how do you do that? You do it by engagement. You do it by planning and sitting down and saying this is what *is* going to happen because in the absence of that information that vacuum will be filled by politicians saying, 'They're going to take your land. They're going to send all the RUC men to jail. They're going to open up tribunals'. Well, somebody has to be able to say sorry, you know, 'The Irish government have signed this international agreement that says the following...'."

Mark's comments have been recognised as sensible. Since that interview took place the Constitutional Unit – based at UCL – has been engaged in working with a range of academic institutions including Ulster University and Dublin City University to consider issues including who would be entitled to vote in a referendum and what questions would be asked.[58]

Philip Gilliland believes we should take the opportunity presented by Brexit to open up the conversation about the constitutional settlement and openly discuss Irish unity. He argues: "We've been given a gift in this process which is called Brexit, because it's allowed those of us who are from a Protestant background, which is me, to be able to talk about the heresy of the united Ireland in a way that is not heresy. It's allowed us to talk about the possibility of constitutional change in a way that doesn't seem to be disloyal

---

"Brexit has clearly changed the dynamic between how we deal with our neighbours in the south and how we deal with our neighbours in Britain."

---

to the tribe, because clearly for many of us, Brexit is nuts. That sounds very disrespectful to people. I should really retract that. People are entitled to their view, if they think it's the right thing to do, brilliant. Fill your boots. That's grand, but it clearly has changed the dynamic between how we deal with our neighbours in the south and how we deal with our neighbours in Britain. It's shone a light on the fact that the British don't really know or care very much about Northern Ireland. We knew that anyway.

"This has shone a light on the fact that those of us whose businesses are totally integrated in the Republic's economy - which mine is - to have a future where that presence in the Irish market is impeded, is a threat to jobs and our livelihoods and so we're going to vote with our economic future.

"It's allowed a lot of us to question, why is it we were unionist in the first place? In the past many of us who were unionist thought we were more socially liberal and there was a fear of theocracy. That's totally changed. We're now the theocrats, apparently. I'm not. I want a socially liberal world. The idea of the socially conservative moral stuff coming out of unionism is utterly abhorrent to me and frankly, ironically, rather un-British too. We've got all sorts of reasons now to talk about the constitutional issue in a way that wasn't open to us.

"Now occasionally when you have conversations with people who you happen to know are Protestants, those sorts of conversations over the last couple of years are actually, 'I don't really care whether we've a united Ireland or not. I just don't want it to be under the heel of Sinn Féin, that's it. If it's

---

58 https://www.ucl.ac.uk/constitution-unit/research/elections-and-referendums/working-group-unification-referendums-island-ireland

not under the heel of Sinn Féin, I don't really care, I'm happy with it. I don't mind.' There's an awful lot more hot air around that issue than people might expect. If there were a border poll and if it were carried, yes there would be some people who would be upset about it, but I don't see it turning into a war, not at all."

It should also be possible to address the day-to-day politics of the Assembly and district councils without having to deal with the constitutional issue. The PUP's John Kyle comments: "People need to have the courage to vote outside of their traditional patterns of voting, particularly in elections where the constitutional issue is not at stake, or is not fundamental to what they're doing."

"When I hear about the push for a border poll in Ireland, I'm just thinking Brexit Part 2."

Clare Bailey adds that the future is about much more than the constitutional arrangements of Northern Ireland – it is also about what might be regarded as 'normal politics', such as wealth distribution and the growing challenge of climate change. She says: "This is a very interesting time to be in politics, just to be alive. We're back into this constitutional notion of are we British, are we Irish? It's that binary sense of who we are. Brexit has brought this up, what will we be the other side of Brexit? Post-Brexit, where there is no plan, we went to a referendum led by hardline Brexiteers with no plan on the table. When I hear about the conversations and the push for a border poll in Ireland, I'm just thinking Brexit Part 2, because there is no plan and that's a real failure from nationalist politicians. If this has been the raison d'être, their whole reason for existence – where is their plan? Where is this Socialist Republic that I have heard about all my days?

"Every economic model that I have seen put forward for the case for unification is built on the same neo-liberal economic system. Is the north just going to be subsumed into the south, are we just going to be one Ireland under Leinster House? These are not fit for purpose conversations. If we want a united Ireland we need to talk about transformation and we need to be in no doubt whatsoever that a new Ireland is coming and she's on her way and she's called climate chaos. So regardless, we've been given 12 years to the point of no return from the International Panel of Climate Change where if we do not radically change our lifestyles, our behaviours, then the damage that will be done will be irreparable. So we are going to be forced into renegotiating who we are on this island, how we get along, what our relationships are, but more importantly how we do business together. I am in no doubt that a new Ireland is coming, but I don't believe that it's the one many people have been thinking of."

She continues: "As climate chaos gathers momentum, as we begin to feel the impact of that more, there is an opportunity to be able to talk about this without it being about an identity, an old school constitutional question, because the future is coming and we have to engage with that. How do we feed ourselves? What is our agricultural output? What are our energy needs? We live on an island and it's quite a small island, surrounded by the Atlantic and the Irish Sea. We have an awful lot of wind, we have mountains. The natural resources that we could be tapping into, not just to produce the energy that we need, but to produce jobs, to produce community wealth, to learn a new way of being. We can be world leaders in this. If we can implement a green new deal[59], we have a proud history of industrial heritage. Belfast was built on it, the shipyards and the industry there. We can use that infrastructure, we can retrain, we can engage, we can create new jobs, long term sustainable jobs investing in new energies and new industries we can build ourselves.

"We have to start looking at new economic models for that within community ownership, co-operatives and small-scale production. There is a huge opportunity that we're going to miss in terms of having those conversations, showing people real possibility outside the narrow nationalist/unionist sense of being where people can thrive within that and it will be sustainable and fit for the future. We need to focus on that. That would be a great way of trying to introduce the possibility of looking to the future."

---

59 The proposed 'green new deal' would invest substantially in low carbon technologies, to reduce carbon emissions.

CONCLUSIONS

THE IDEAS

The purpose of this book is to highlight the ideas put forward by a range of opinion leaders on how we can make progress in Northern Ireland, embedding the peace process and improving the quality of life across the population. While the focus is on Northern Ireland, the impact would also be on the border region and in the rest of the Irish Republic.

We are not trying to suggest that every idea warrants acceptance and implementation. Rather that it is worth discussing and considering ideas that have been put forward by people who have thought seriously about Northern Ireland's problems, often with the benefit of being inside the system at senior levels.

The ideas warrant consideration – there needs to be more thoughtful debate about our future.

In addition, the Holywell Trust has a long and respected role in building community engagement and reconciliation. Previous programmes have themselves concluded with proposals for positive change, which are also included below.

LEADERSHIP

- Everyone involved in politics and governance in Northern Ireland should regularly re-read the Good Friday Agreement and re-affirm their commitment to its core principles.

- Accept we are mid-way into a peace project that will last at least 50 years. This means avoiding unrealistic expectations in the short term and being committed to staying with the process into the long term.

- Focus on putting in place structures of good governance.

- Make faster progress in establishing a series of Citizens' Assemblies to address the big problems facing Northern Ireland, including fundamental public sector reform and health service reform, considering the Bengoa proposals. Set-up some small scale neighbourhood-based Citizens' Assemblies to address local problems such as reducing tension in interface areas. If preferred, they could be called People's Assemblies.

- Consider the opportunities for health service integration on a cross-border basis, to improve health outcomes, reduce costs and increase access to specialist services.

- Review the arrangements of the Good Friday Agreement in terms of designation. The current workings of the GFA discriminate against parties such as the Green Party and the Alliance Party.
- Adopt a truth and reconciliation process that learns from South Africa.
- Recognise that any form of comprehensive justice is now impossible and that attempts to take action through prosecutions can at this stage cause enormous hurt and suffering. Honesty about the past may be more important and relevant now than seeking retribution.
- Political parties need to consider and acknowledge past roles in causing hurt, pain and in, some cases, deaths. It was not only those who used the gun or the bomb that have some responsibility for what happened in the Troubles, but also those who cheered on their tribe.
- Initiate a 'Bengoa-type' review of the education system, focused on strengthening relationships across the sectoral divides within education (both those based on religion and between selective and non-selective schools), reducing costs and improving outcomes. This is likely to involve school mergers, could involve the creation of cross-community sixth form colleges in place of existing school sixth forms.
- Encourage the development of 'civic unionism', in the same way that 'civic nationalism' has been established – and move beyond that to promote discussions between civic unionism and civic nationalism.
- Enact a Bill of Rights, as expected from the Good Friday Agreement.
- Take firm action against paramilitary flags and insignia, particularly close to shared housing areas and integrated schools.
- End funding for groups connected with active paramilitaries.
- Promote open debate to decide what outcomes would be possible in future referenda.
- Support the work of academic institutions in considering the wording of future referenda on the constitutional arrangements in Ireland, who would be entitled to vote in them and in what circumstances referenda would be called.
- Hold open conversations about constitutional arrangements for the future of Ireland, both north and south. Be generous and inclusive.

- Encourage the media to avoid deliberately stoking communal division.
- Promote the responsible use of social media.
- Recognise the value, and need, for compromise in public life.
- Publicise the cost of segregation through service duplication as a means of gaining public support for public sector reform.

SHARING SOCIETY

- Politicians to fully engage with people and parties from other traditions, recognising that engagement is not a defeat.
- Learn from the success of resolving parading disputes in Derry and the replacement of the RUC, through community dialogue.
- Move towards other forms of local democratic engagement, including participative budgeting. This might help to address the democratic deficit of low voter turnout.
- Put more resources and publicity on increasing the size of the electoral register, with the aim of increasing voter engagement and turn-out.
- Establish structural methods that promote reconciliation. This might involve the creation of a Department for Reconciliation, or else monitor all government spending through the PASS (Policy Appraisal for Sharing over Separation) process. Substantially increase spending on reconciliation, funded through public sector efficiency savings.
- Engage in processes in which political representatives and other citizens consider what rights they would want if they belonged to a different community, attempting to build empathy.
- Promote events that support reconciliation and emotional recovery. Promote church and sporting attendance that cross the traditional divide.
- Recognise women's groups engaged in cross-community work and ensure they receive sufficient funds to continue and expand their work.
- Allocate more funding to cross-community youth groups, including at interface areas.
- Respect the role of the community sector, as service providers, as voices for their community, as key actors for social cohesion and reconciliation.
- Encourage voters from the two main traditions to consider not only who they want in government from their own tradition, but also who they want to share power with.

- Make urgent progress with the Oral History Archive, while people are still alive to contribute. Ensure the archive focuses on the commonality of the experiences of the Troubles, including the pain of loss, avoiding the stoking of divisions.

- Establish a 'Day of Acknowledgement', or other processes by which pain of loss is recognised. Consider the lessons of international experience, such as Holocaust remembrance and Hiroshima.

- Invest substantially in mental health services, recognising the crisis in Northern Ireland.

- Recognise the inter-generational impact of the Troubles and of the related mental ill-health.

- Commit to a major expansion of shared housing provision, based on the building of city centre apartment buildings (e.g. in Belfast and Derry). This may be more successful in building shared communities than new build estates, particularly those close to existing interface lines, which are subject to paramilitary intimidation.

- Create a body to promote shared housing.

- Strengthen partnerships between non-selective post-primary schools and local grammar schools, increasing opportunities for pupils at non-selective schools.

- Invest in a new generation of Sure Start pre-school facilities, enabling children to mix across divides before they start schooling.

- Expand the higher education sector in Northern Ireland, to improve the skills base and strengthen social cohesion.

- Sustained leadership training programmes should be agreed, established and developed in all post-primary schools, aimed at the 14 to 18 years age group.

- Recognise the value of the arts in addressing social and political challenges and in making positive contributions to social integration through reconciliation and shared experiences.

- Encourage the development of 'the new story of social healing' based on the work of John Paul Lederach.

- Training programmes should be developed to enhance negotiation and dispute reconciliation skills.

- Pilot projects of integrated city and town centre housing schemes should be developed across Northern Ireland in city and town centres. These might replace some existing commercial developments that no longer fit modern retailing demand – such as the Richmond Centre in Derry.

- Promote projects which engage young people in exploring local responses to the threats from climate change.

- Develop environmental volunteering programmes which are cross-community, such as Connswater, and cross-border, for example at Strabane/Lifford.

- Develop programmes which encourage young people to explore answers to problems in other countries, such as food security and climate change impacts, in association with local universities and further education colleges.

BUILDING A PROSPEROUS SOCIETY

- Adopt an effective strategy to address deprivation and exclusion. There is a clear and demonstrated linkage between deprivation and exclusion on one hand and the allure of paramilitaries on the other. Even Belfast, whose economy has grown strongly in recent years, contains areas in West, North and East Belfast of significant deprivation, little touched in terms of improved employment outcomes. This is also true of the North West, with even higher levels of economic inactivity. More investment in skills and infrastructure will help address these problems, but a comprehensive strategy is required. The Good Friday Agreement has not delivered significant social and economic benefits for much of the population: this failure endangers the peace.

- Promote positive role models, particularly in deprived communities, supporting young people from deprived communities to succeed.

- Improve vocational education and apprenticeship opportunities for pupils disenchanted with, or disconnected from, their schools.

- Begin career guidance at an early stage in post-primary education, to build pupils' aspirations.

- Encourage national investment in wealth creation potential of wind/water and natural power production using the example of the Norwegian sovereign wealth fund.

INDEX